THE BOOK OF
TIME

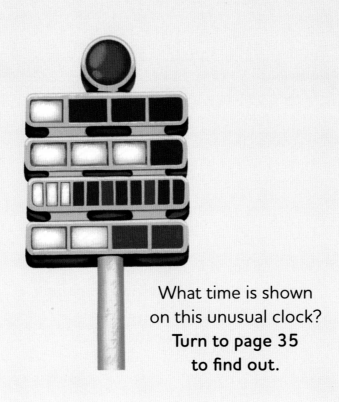

What time is shown
on this unusual clock?
Turn to page 35
to find out.

© 2023 Quarto Publishing plc
Clive Gifford © 2023
Teo Georgiev © 2023

First published in 2023 by words & pictures,
an imprint of The Quarto Group.
1 Triptych Place, London,
SE1 9SH, United Kingdom.
T (0)20 7700 6700 F (0)20 7700 8066
www.quarto.com

Editor: Claire Saunders
Art Director: Susi Martin
Associate Publisher: Holly Willsher

A catalogue record for this book is available from the British Library.

ISBN: 978-0-7112-7955-1

9 8 7 6 5 4 3 2 1

Printed in Malaysia COS042023

THE BOOK OF
TIME

ADVENTURES IN THE PAST, PRESENT, FUTURE AND BEYOND

How long did a day last in the time of the dinosaurs? **Discover the answer on page 16.**

CLIVE GIFFORD
ILLUSTRATED BY
TEO GEORGIEV

words & pictures

CONTENTS

ABOUT TIME!

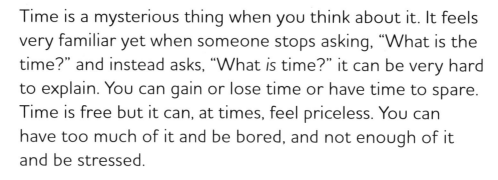

Time is a mysterious thing when you think about it. It feels very familiar yet when someone stops asking, "What is the time?" and instead asks, "What *is* time?" it can be very hard to explain. You can gain or lose time or have time to spare. Time is free but it can, at times, feel priceless. You can have too much of it and be bored, and not enough of it and be stressed.

You cannot touch, taste or smell time, but you can feel it passing. And although each minute, hour and day are exactly the same length, you can feel some pass far more quickly or slowly than others.

Time has been worshipped and studied, used as a tool and sold as a product, caused riots and made people's fortunes. This book looks at how time has been harnessed in history and some of the wild ways people kept track of time in the past. It shows how advances in measuring time changed the world and introduces some time titans who saved time, as well as those who wasted and tinkered with it.

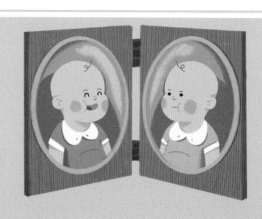

You'll learn how time varies in different places, how time is used to uncover the past and how people's views of time have changed, ahem, over time.

Along the way you'll learn answers to questions including:

- When did time begin?
- Will it ever end?
- Do animals feel time like we do?
- Is time the same on other planets?
- Why are some people always late?
- What's the smallest unit of time?
- Is time travel possible?
- What's the biggest clock?
- Was there really a 445-day year?

And there's even the chance to become a record breaker...

... if you have the time!

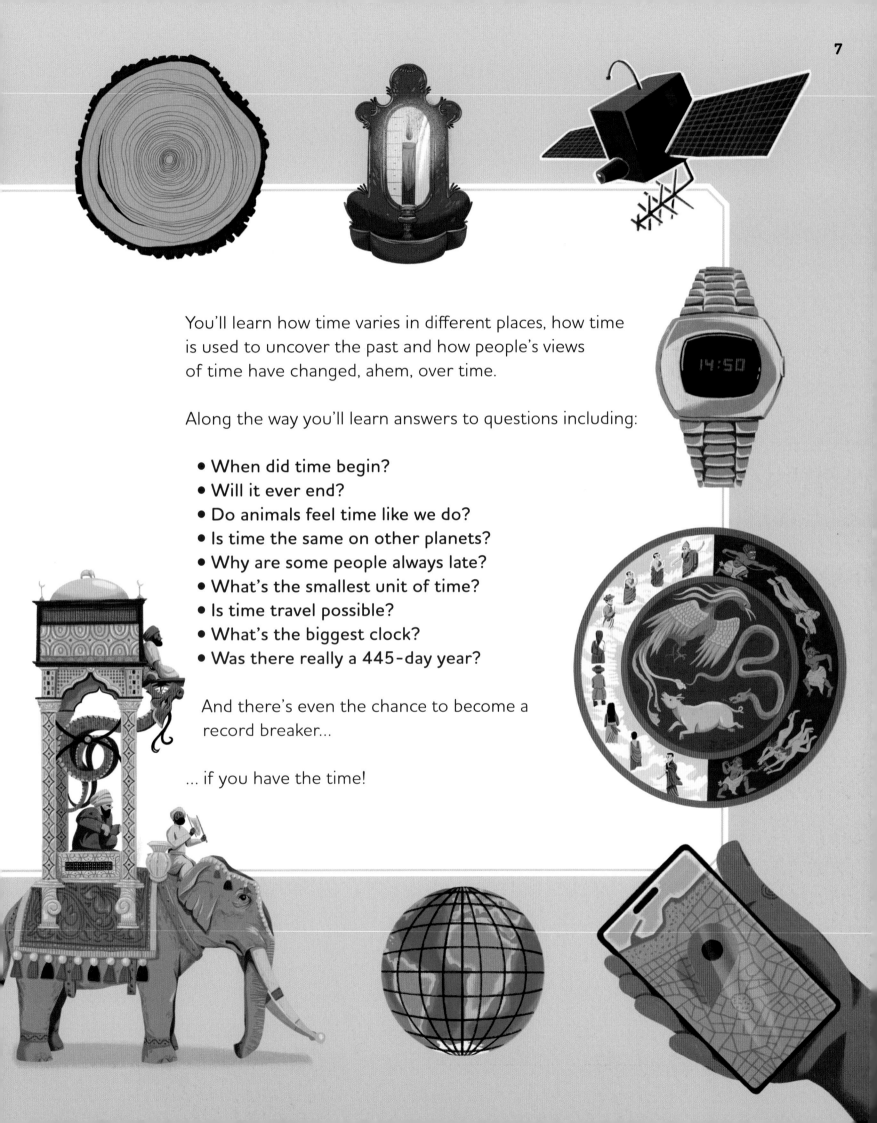

EVERYDAY TIME

Every day, our lives are influenced by time, even when we're not wearing a watch or carrying a smartphone. Time is in action all around us, from making cars and computers work to delivering goods and services and helping keep us safe.

Many sports rely on time, from cycling time trials and timed playing periods in football, to runners trying to beat their best time over a set distance.

Factories rely on 'just-in-time' manufacturing where stocks of raw materials or parts are delivered just before they're needed on the assembly line.

The length of time that traffic lights stay red or green is sometimes altered to let traffic flow more smoothly.

Timetables set out the school day so students know where they should be when. School hours vary between countries. The school day in Taiwan starts at 7.30am for some chidren and lasts up to 9 ½ hours.

People rely on the scheduled services of trains, trams and buses to get to where they're going on time. LED screens and apps will often display when the next service is due to arrive.

NEXT BUS 2mins

BIG TIME

Ten years is a decade, a hundred years is a century and a thousand years is a millennium... but there are far bigger units of time used by scientists. Cosmic or cosmological time is the biggest of all. It is the timespan used to describe the entire history of the Universe.

Cosmic Calendar

For centuries and centuries, most people believed the Earth and the Universe was merely thousands not billions of years old.

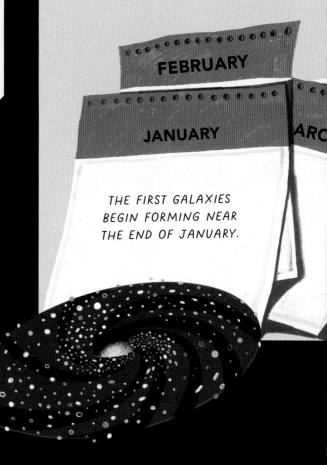

THE FIRST GALAXIES BEGIN FORMING NEAR THE END OF JANUARY.

Cosmic Time

The Universe is everything we know about, from the smallest atom to the biggest galaxy. We believe it began with a HUGE expansion of space and matter from a single point. This event is known as the Big Bang and scientists reckon it happened about 13.77 billion years ago, plus or minus 40 million years. When you're dealing with billions, a few million is a pretty good margin of error!

Scientists believe that there was no 'before' the Big Bang in our Universe, only after. Why? Because time was created at the same moment as matter and space.

13.77 BILLION YEARS AGO (BYA):
THE BIG BANG BEGINS! AFTER JUST
1 MILLIONTH OF A SECOND, THE UNIVERSE
WAS RED HOT – 10,000,000,000 °C

12.7 BYA:
LARGE NUMBERS OF STAR
AND GALAXIES FORM

13.7 BYA:
THE UNIVERSE IS DARK, WITH
NO LIGHT, STARS OR GALAXIES

We now know that isn't the case and also, that Earth is a relative latecomer to the Universe party.

One way of showing this is the Cosmic Calendar, which squeezes all of cosmic time into a single Earth calendar year. The Big Bang signals the start of 1st January.

THE DISC OF THE MILKY WAY (OUR GALAXY) BEGINS FORMING IN MAY.

MAY

JUNE

JULY

AUGU

SEPTEMBER

EARTH DOESN'T APPEAR UNTIL SEPTEMBER.

TOBER

NOVEMBER

DECEMBER

PLANTS ON LAND DON'T TURN UP UNTIL 20TH DECEMBER OR SO.

THE FIRST DINOSAURS ARRIVE ON 24TH OR 25TH DECEMBER...

... AND ANCIENT EGYPTIANS BUILD THE PYRAMIDS AT 12 SECONDS TO MIDNIGHT IN THE FINAL MINUTE OF NEW YEAR'S EVE.

9.7 BYA: THE UNIVERSE IS ABOUT ONE-THIRD OF ITS PRESENT SIZE

4.6 BYA: OUR SOLAR SYSTEM (THE SUN AND ITS NEIGHBOURING PLANETS) BEGINS TO FORM

245–66 MILLION YEARS AGO (MYA): THE AGE OF THE DINOSAURS

ABOUT 320,000 YEARS AGO: THE FIRST MODERN HUMANS APPEAR

Back in Time

Light takes a long time to travel through the vast Universe to reach Earth. When we see a star that is 1 million light years away, the view we get is of how it looked 1 million years ago. So, all our views of space are looking back in time.

SO, THE UNIVERSE IS 1,377,000,000 DECADES, 137,700,000 CENTURIES OR 13.77 GA OLD. GA IS SHORT FOR A GIGA-ANNUM OR ONE BILLION YEARS

SMALL TIME

In fast sports, competitors may be timed to tenths, hundredths, even thousandths of a second. But split-second measurements of time don't stop there. They get smaller and smaller.

Milliseconds

Let's start with the smallest unit of time on a stopwatch. A millisecond is just 1/1000th (0.001) of a second, but a lot can go on within even a few of these. In just 11 milliseconds, for example, your body will shed five or six skin cells, whilst a millisecond pulsar (a spinning star in space) will turn 360 degrees, a task it takes Earth 24 hours to achieve.

In 40–70 milliseconds, a car can register that a crash is happening and inflate its airbag, protecting the driver from head and chest injuries.

It takes around 160–190 milliseconds for a sprinter to react to the starter's pistol and begin to race.

In 400 milliseconds, a baseball can travel from the pitcher's hand to reach the bat. Whoosh!

Microseconds

One microsecond is a millionth (0.000001) of a second. To get across just how small a unit of time this is, a blink of an eye can take 150,000 microseconds. Some pretty explosive things happen in a handful of microseconds. These include a stick of dynamite exploding (24 microseconds) and a party balloon popping (10 microseconds).

Nanoseconds

A nanosecond is 1 billionth (0.000000001) of a second. Blink and you've missed millions of them! The atomic clocks found inside GPS satellites (see p.40) are accurate to within 3 nanoseconds.

In 1 nanosecond, light travels about 29.9 cm – around the length of a ruler.

Picoseconds

This is a trillionth (0.000000000001) of a second or, put another way, a millionth of a millionth of a second. Light can travel from the Earth to just past the Moon in $1\frac{1}{4}$ seconds, but in $1\frac{1}{4}$ picoseconds, it travels less than 0.4 mm!

You'd think nothing is worth measuring in such tiny units but you'd be wrong – lasers, radio frequencies and the speed at which computers work can all be measured in picoseconds. For instance, a high-powered computer with a 4.5Ghz processor takes 222 picoseconds to add two numbers together.

Femtoseconds

We're getting mind-blowingly small now – just 0.000000000000001th of a second! There are 1,000 femtoseconds in a picosecond. At these miniscule units of time, you can see the atoms in molecules of substances actually vibrate to and fro. Chemists use lasers to measure some chemical reactions in femtoseconds.

Even Smaller

In 2020, German scientists succeeded in measuring something in an even tinier unit of time. A zeptosecond is **1 million times** smaller than a femtosecond. It takes 247 zeptoseconds for light to travel across a single molecule of hydrogen.

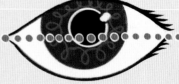

When light reaches your eye, it only takes around 200 femtoseconds for the light-detecting cells at the back of your eye to react.

THE YEAR AND SEASONS

A lot of our everyday time, like days and years, is based on how our planet moves through space. Earth's no slouch. It whizzes along on its orbit around the Sun at a speedy 29.78 km every second. That's 107,208 km/hour −335 times faster than a Formula One racing car!

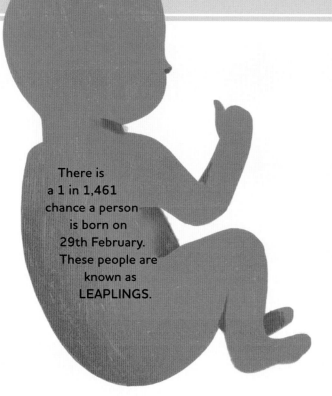

There is a 1 in 1,461 chance a person is born on 29th February. These people are known as LEAPLINGS.

Leaping Ahead

Earth may race through space but it still takes 365.242189 days to complete one orbit of the Sun. That 1/242189th of a day causes a bit of a headache. It means our year of 365 calendar days is slightly out of sync with how long it takes Earth to complete a whole orbit. To get in sync, we have leap years, where we add an extra day to the shortest month once every 4 years. This 'intercalary' or leap day is always 29th February.

Leap years are actually a teensy bit more complicated than that. We actually need 97 leap years every 400 years to sync our calendar with Earth's orbit, not 100. This means any year that is exactly divisible by 100 isn't a leap year... unless it is exactly divisible by 400. Told you it was complicated! So, the year 2000 was a leap year, but 2100 won't be.

Big Impact

In many parts of the world, the year is split up into seasons, each with different weather conditions and temperatures. This reason we have seasons is thanks to an event that took place around 4.5 billion years ago. Earth was an infant when a mystery object, which scientists named Theia, collided with it. CRASH!

Earth was knocked off balance and gained quite a lean. As a result, our planet travels through space not with its North Pole exactly at the top, but tilted at a jaunty angle of 23.4 degrees. This angle doesn't change throughout the year, but how Earth faces the Sun as it orbits does.

Theia's impact with Earth threw up lots of matter into space. Many scientists believe that this all clumped together to form the Moon.

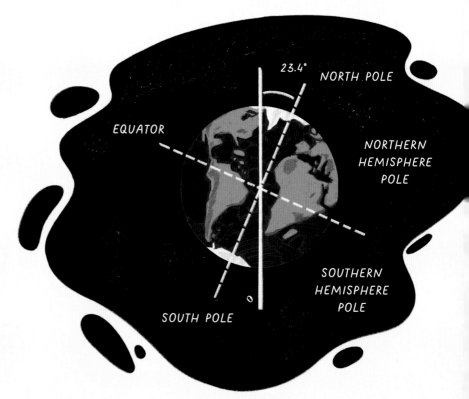

23.4° NORTH POLE

EQUATOR

NORTHERN HEMISPHERE POLE

SOUTHERN HEMISPHERE POLE

SOUTH POLE

Changing Seasons

Earth can be split into two hemispheres or halves, either side of the equator, which is the imaginary line that runs around the centre of the Earth. As our planet orbits the Sun, its tilt means that one or the other hemisphere will be tilted more towards the Sun and receive more of its energy.

For example, in June, July and August, the North Pole is tilted more towards the Sun, meaning the northern hemisphere receives more energy and enjoys summer. When it's summer in the north, it's winter in the south. The southern hemisphere is tilted away from the Sun, receives less energy, is colder and experiences its winter. The roles reverse during the southern hemisphere's summer.

Not everywhere experiences four seasons each year. There is barely any change in climate for those living on or close to the equator, as the Earth's tilt doesn't occur there. Many of these equatorial regions divide their year into two seasons: a long, dry season, and a shorter season when the rains come.

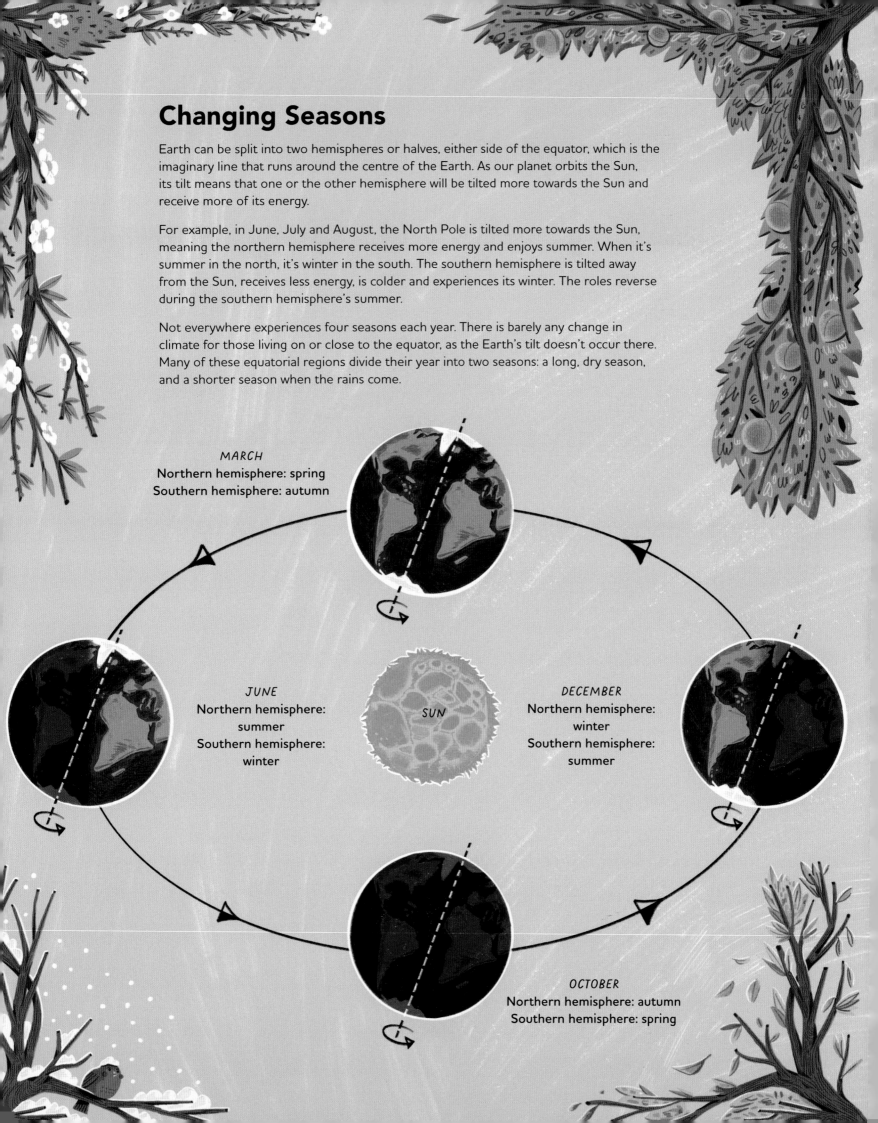

MARCH
Northern hemisphere: spring
Southern hemisphere: autumn

JUNE
Northern hemisphere:
summer
Southern hemisphere:
winter

SUN

DECEMBER
Northern hemisphere:
winter
Southern hemisphere:
summer

OCTOBER
Northern hemisphere: autumn
Southern hemisphere: spring

LONG DAY?

Some days may feel longer than others, like a day spent doing chores compared to a day at a theme park. But all days are pretty much the same length. An Earth day hasn't always been 24 hours long, though, and there have not always been 365 of them in a year.

Dino Days

Back in the time of the dinosaurs, days were a little shorter and there were more of them. Around 68 million years ago, T. Rex would have experienced days that were 23 $\frac{1}{2}$ hours long, with 372 of them in a year.

Going still further back in time, days were even shorter. Around 600 million years ago, they lasted round 21 hours and years were more than 410 days long.

If we go even further back to about 1.4 billion years ago, a day lasted just 18.7 hours and there were 470 of them in a year. How was that possible? It's all down to Earth spinning round faster in the past.

In a Spin

The planet you're standing on is not just moving through space on its orbit around the Sun. It's also spinning round like a top, and fast, too. At the equator, it turns at about 1,670 km/hour – almost twice the speed of a jet airliner. We don't feel this because we're moving at the same rate with it. Earth's rotation gives rise to day and night.

Earth spins anticlockwise on its axis.

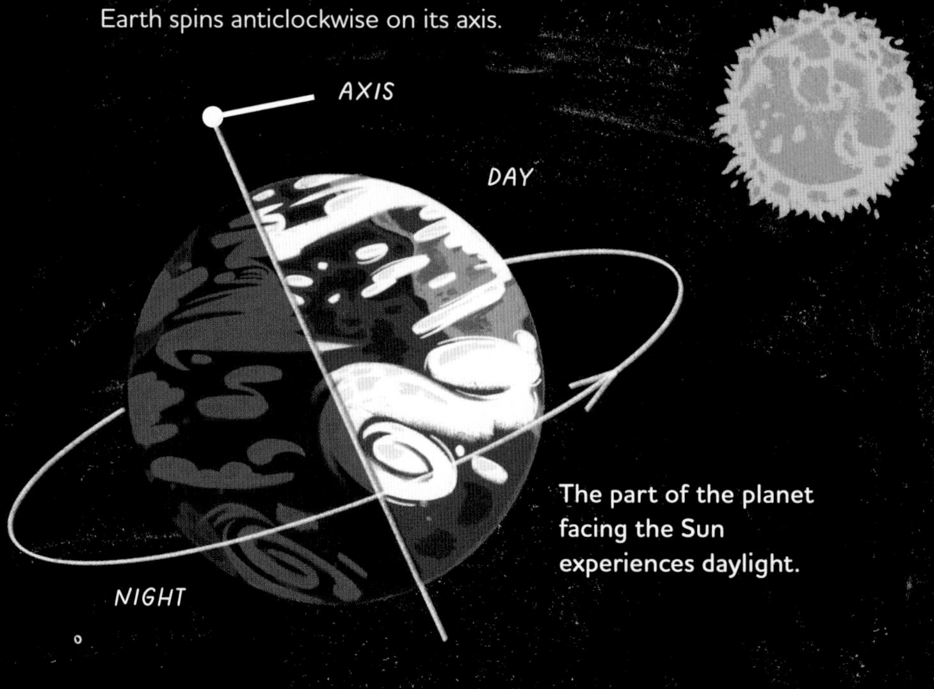

Earth completes a full 360° spin every 86,400 seconds (24 hours) on average.

The part of the planet facing the Sun experiences daylight.

Brake Time

So why did Earth spin faster in the past? It's partly down to our nearest neighbour in space. The Moon orbits Earth due to the pull of Earth's gravity (the pulling force of attraction between objects). But the Moon, although much smaller than Earth, exerts its own gravity in return.

The Moon's gravity pulls at water across Earth's surface, helping to create high and low tides. The moving high tide around the planet is called a tidal bulge, and the spinning Earth loses energy trying to drag the bulge along with it. This causes our planet to slow down its spinning speed, ever so slightly.

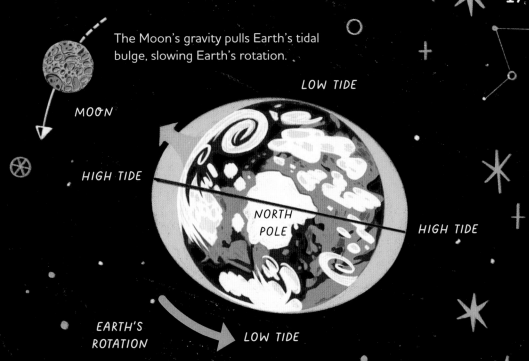

The Moon's gravity pulls Earth's tidal bulge, slowing Earth's rotation.

MOON

LOW TIDE

HIGH TIDE

NORTH POLE

HIGH TIDE

EARTH'S ROTATION

LOW TIDE

As a result, the days are getting fractionally longer, but only by 1.7 milliseconds (0.0017 seconds) every 100 years. So, don't get excited about having to wait fewer days between birthdays! It will take 200 million years to get to a 25-hour day and 350-day year.

23:59:59

SNOOZE

At your Service

The speed of Earth's spin is monitored by an organisation called the International Earth Rotation and Reference Systems Service (IERS), based in Paris. This agency decides when it's time to adjust the clocks to keep in sync with Earth's changing spin speed.

In 2016, the IERS added a cheeky leap second to the world's clocks at the very end of the year. This made 2016 a second longer than other years.

Leap seconds are added at midnight on either 30th June or 31st December. Since 1972, 27 leap seconds have been added.

TIME IN SPACE

As Earthlings, when we head out into space to explore, we measure everything in terms of Earth days, years and hours. But what are days and years like on neighbouring planets and what's time like for astronauts in space?

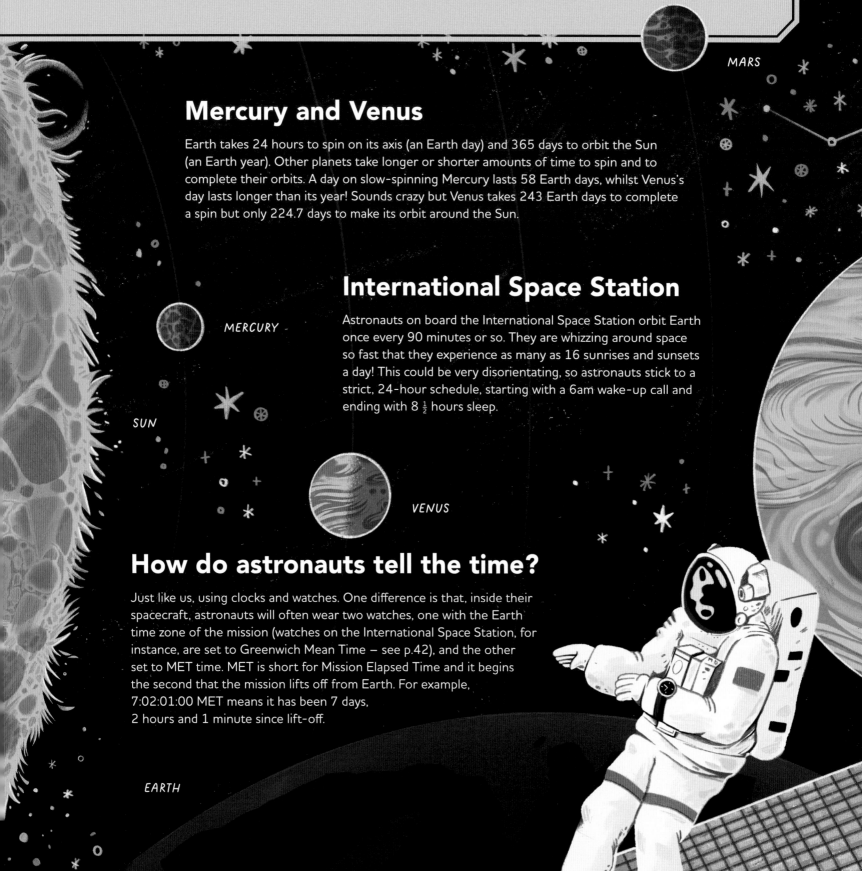

Mercury and Venus

Earth takes 24 hours to spin on its axis (an Earth day) and 365 days to orbit the Sun (an Earth year). Other planets take longer or shorter amounts of time to spin and to complete their orbits. A day on slow-spinning Mercury lasts 58 Earth days, whilst Venus's day lasts longer than its year! Sounds crazy but Venus takes 243 Earth days to complete a spin but only 224.7 days to make its orbit around the Sun.

International Space Station

Astronauts on board the International Space Station orbit Earth once every 90 minutes or so. They are whizzing around space so fast that they experience as many as 16 sunrises and sunsets a day! This could be very disorientating, so astronauts stick to a strict, 24-hour schedule, starting with a 6am wake-up call and ending with 8 ½ hours sleep.

MARS

MERCURY

SUN

VENUS

How do astronauts tell the time?

Just like us, using clocks and watches. One difference is that, inside their spacecraft, astronauts will often wear two watches, one with the Earth time zone of the mission (watches on the International Space Station, for instance, are set to Greenwich Mean Time — see p.42), and the other set to MET time. MET is short for Mission Elapsed Time and it begins the second that the mission lifts off from Earth. For example, 7:02:01:00 MET means it has been 7 days, 2 hours and 1 minute since lift-off.

EARTH

Mars

Earth isn't the only planet to be tilted, producing seasons (see p.14). Mars also has changing weather conditions throughout the year, due to its tilt of 25 degrees — similar to our own planet. Whilst there are no live Martian creatures to observe, astronomers do watch the planet's polar ice caps, which shrink in summer and grow in winter. As Mars takes almost twice as long as Earth to orbit the Sun — 687 days to be precise — the seasons on Mars also last twice as long.

Jupiter

You could fit 1,300 Earths inside Jupiter. For such a big ball of gas, it sure is a fast mover, spinning as fast as 43,000 km/h. This means its day is the shortest of the solar system planets, lasting just 9 hours, 50 minutes at its equator.

JUPITER

Neptune

If you're a fan of birthdays, be relieved you don't live on Neptune. Apart from it being a desperately chilly place with no solid surface (because it's a big ball of gas), it takes Neptune around 165 Earth years to complete its orbit. This means you'd never enjoy a birthday.

Uranus

When it comes to tilt, no planet beats Uranus. It lies on its side at an angle of 98 degrees. As a result, in summer, one pole of Uranus plus a large section of that pole's hemisphere directly faces the Sun continuously for 21 years. Meanwhile, the wintry half stays in darkness for 21 years. Temperatures plummet as low as -224.2 °C — the coldest in the solar system. Brrrr!

URANUS

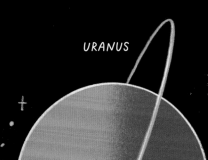

HIGH IN THE SKY

Prehistoric people could hardly fail to notice and study the giant glowing orb that brought warmth and light each day. They tracked the Sun's path across the sky and learned how its precise position varied with the passing of time.

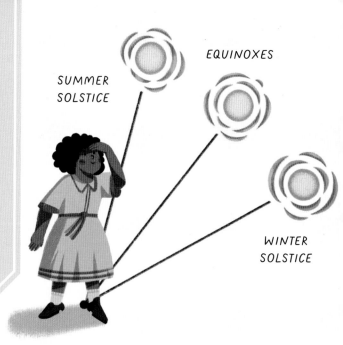

SUMMER SOLSTICE

EQUINOXES

WINTER SOLSTICE

Noon or midday (12:00) is the point at which the Sun is at its highest in the sky every day. This height changes throughout the year.

Solstices and Equinoxes

The summer solstice is the day on which the Sun is highest in the sky all year. In the northern hemisphere, this is most commonly on 21st June. In the southern hemisphere it's most commonly 21st December. The summer solstice marks the shortest night and longest day of the year.

The winter solstice is usually 21st December in the northern hemisphere and 21st June in the southern. The Sun is at its lowest point at midday all year, and the result is the shortest day of the year with less daylight than any other.

Equinoxes can be thought of as halfway points between solstices, where the length of day and night are equal. These occur in March (the vernal equinox) and September (the autumnal equinox).

Midsummer and Midwinter Monuments

Early peoples managed to construct some astonishing monuments that lined up with the Sun's movements each year. The Newgrange tomb in Ireland was built over 5,000 years ago. It is perfectly aligned so that on the winter solstice, the Sun rises and shines directly down a 19-metre-long narrow passage to light up the stone burial chamber in the centre.

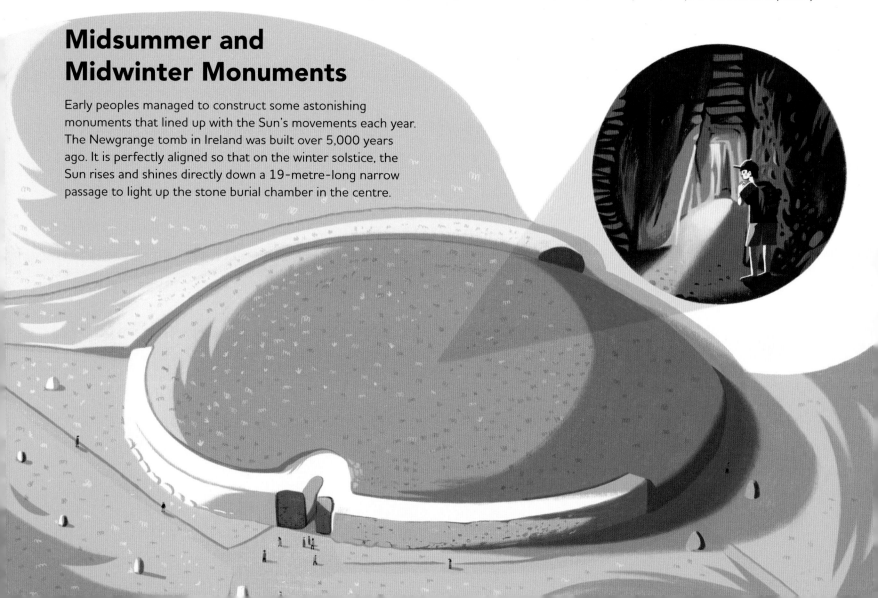

Stonehenge

This giant stone circle in England, built more than 4,000 years ago, was a triumph of ancient engineering and early Sun-watching. At the summer solstice, the Sun rises behind a 30-tonne rock called the Heel Stone, some 77 m away from the centre of the circle. The Sun's rays then shine on the Altar Stone in the centre of the circle.

Stonehenge's stones also align with when the Sun sets at the winter solstice. The last sunlight of that day passed through a trilithon – a structure made of one giant stone resting like a crossbar on two stone uprights.

ALTAR STONE

Solstice Celebrations

The winter solstice was a cause for celebration, as from that point in midwinter, days would start getting longer. Some prehistoric farming peoples in Europe, such as the Celts, welcomed both solstices by lighting bonfires. They thought that the bonfires' flames would help boost the Sun's energy and see it return strongly for the next growing season.

Chankillo

This 2,300-year-old monument in Peru is made up of 13 stone towers regularly spaced along a hill for almost 300 m. Viewed from an observation platform, each tower lines up with the sunrise for 10 days. The people who built this monument are thought to have divided up their time into 10-day weeks. The Sun lines up with the end two towers at the solstices, and with the middle tower at the equinoxes – ingenious!

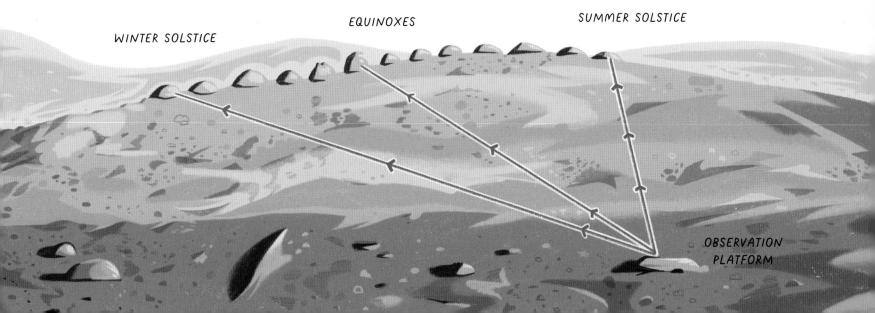

WINTER SOLSTICE

EQUINOXES

SUMMER SOLSTICE

OBSERVATION PLATFORM

TIME OF DAY

Whilst early humans could count the number of days passed, they had no way of tracking the passage of time through a day. As civilisations developed, so did the first ways of telling the time.

MIDDAY

MID-MORNING

SUNRISE

Shadowy Stuff

When people stuck a straight stick, later called a gnomon, vertically in the ground, they could study the shadow cast by the Sun. The shadow was longest at sunrise when the Sun was low in the sky, and grew gradually shorter until midday, after which it grew longer again until sunset.

Early civilisations like the Sumerians and Egyptians lived under mostly cloudless skies, and were the first to tell the time in this way, often using tall, slender stone pillars called obelisks. The Egyptians later added a dial at the base of their obelisks or gnomons, with markings dividing the day up into shorter units of time. Eventually this became the sundial, and its use spread all over the world.

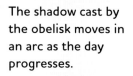

The shadow cast by the obelisk moves in an arc as the day progresses.

No Sun? No Problem!

Sundials were all very well, but what happens when it's overcast or dark? People began inventing alternatives. Sandglasses, which measured the flow of sand through the narrow neck of a glass container, proved portable and popular. These could be filled with any time-unit of sand, but hourglasses (measuring an hour) became the most popular.

Burning Issue

The ancient Chinese invented candle clocks almost 2,000 years ago. As a burning candle gradually melted, markings on the candle or on an engraved scale showed how much time had passed. Typically, candle clocks only lasted 4–6 hours so had to be replaced regularly.

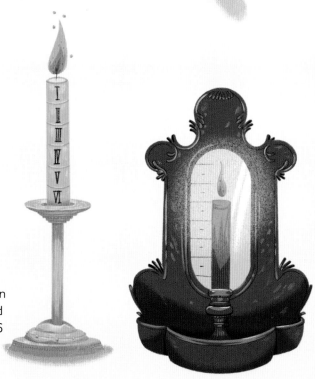

Ancient Incense Clock

Ancient Chinese, Indian and Japanese timekeepers invented ingenious incense clocks. These burned through threads tied to metal bells, causing them to fall with a jingle every hour or so. Others burned trails of different 'flavours' of powdered incense, so you didn't have to see or hear the time, but could smell it changing!

Water Works

Water clocks used the flow of water to tell the time. Ancient Babylonians and Greeks pioneered these clocks, sometimes called clepsydras, meaning 'water thieves'. In India, copper bowls called ghatis were drilled with a hole that allowed them, when placed in a basin of water, to fill in around 24 minutes (we say around, as these simple water clocks weren't terribly accurate). At the time, India divided its day into 24-minute blocks, 60 of them!

AL-JAZARI'S
ELEPHANT
WATER CLOCK

Clocks Get Complex

In China and the Muslim world, gifted engineers used the flow of water to power very elaborate mechanical machines. Around 1200, Muslim engineer Al-Jazari designed enormous water clocks in the shapes of elephants and castles, with water powering ropes, gears and levers to move the clocks' parts. These included serpents that swallowed metal balls, and moving mechanical figures that played drums and trumpets – quite a sight... and sound!

ANCIENT
BABYLONIAN
WATER CLOCK

CURIOUS CALENDARS

As early peoples learned how the Sun and Moon moved and how the seasons repeated in a regular cycle, they developed calendars as a way of keeping track of time. Lots of different civilisations meant lots of different calendars!

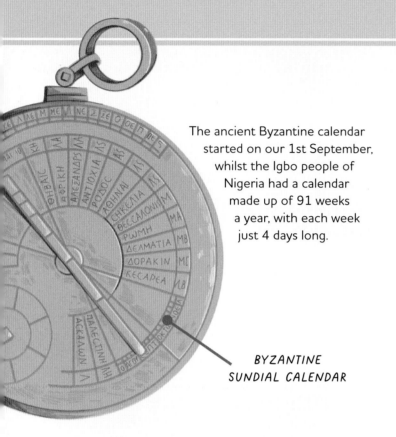

The ancient Byzantine calendar started on our 1st September, whilst the Igbo people of Nigeria had a calendar made up of 91 weeks a year, with each week just 4 days long.

BYZANTINE SUNDIAL CALENDAR

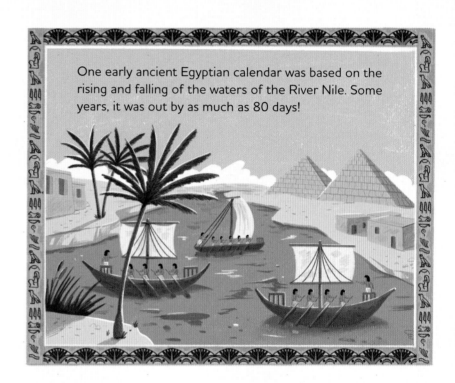

One early ancient Egyptian calendar was based on the rising and falling of the waters of the River Nile. Some years, it was out by as much as 80 days!

Mayan Months

More than 2,000 years ago, the Maya of Central America developed not one but three calendars. The shortest, **Tzolk'in**, lasted 260 days. The **Haab** calendar started in July and lasted 365 days split into 18 months, each 20 days long. The 5 leftover days formed a mini month called *Uayeb*, which was thought to be extremely unlucky. Best stay in!

The Maya's third calendar was a far longer-term measure of time called the **Long Count**. Archaeologists think it lasted 2,880,000 days, at the end of which the Maya believed the Universe was destroyed and re-created.

UAYEB

SOTS – THE FOURTH MONTH, REPRESENTED BY A BAT

XUL – THE SIXTH MONTH, REPRESENTED BY A DOG

THIS HAAB CALENDAR DISC SHOWS THE 18 MAYAN MONTHS AND UAYEB – THE UNLUCKY 19TH MONTH.

New Year, New Fire

The Aztecs used similar 260-day and 365-day calendars to the Maya who came before them. The two calendars align perfectly once every 52 years, when the Aztecs would perform *Toxhiuhmolpilia* or the New Fire ceremony. All fires around the Aztec's empire were put out, and an unfortunate person was killed as a sacrifice to the god of fire, Xiuhtecuhtli. A fire was then lit in their chest, from which other fires could be lit to fire up the empire again!

The Longest Year

The ancient Roman calendar began in March each year. By 46 BCE it was in a mess, months out of sync with the seasons. Julius Caesar ordered a new 365.25-day 'Julian' calendar that started in January, with a leap year every 4 years. Brilliant! But to get in sync for the following year, Caesar had to add an extra 3 months to 46 BCE, making it the longest year Rome had known – 445 days! This led to confusion over food, religious festivals, taxes and more besides. The Julian calendar would, however, be used throughout Europe for 1,600 years.

All our month names stem from the Romans, who named them after their gods, rulers or the month's position in the year. The month Julius (July) was named in Caesar's honour.

JANUARY IS NAMED AFTER THE ROMAN GOD JANUS, WITH TWO FACES LOOKING BACK AND FORWARDS.

The Great Change

Caesar's Julian calendar wasn't perfect. By 1582, it was 10 days adrift of the seasons, and Pope Gregory XIII declared a switch to a new 'Gregorian' calendar. Catholic countries mostly adopted the new calendar straight away but others took some convincing. Britain didn't switch until 1752, by which time the old calendar was 11 days out of sync with the new one. To correct this, Brits went to bed on 2nd September, but woke up on the 14th. Many people were outraged and convinced that their lives had been shortened!

Calendar confusion still occurred even into the 20th century. In 1908, the Russian Olympic shooting team, using the old Julian calendar, turned up to the London Games 12 days late and missed their events! Russia didn't start using the Gregorian calendar until 1918, China in 1912 and Greece in 1923.

TIME IN CULTURE

Time influences many parts of culture, from superstitions to celebrations of time passing. Many religions and faiths have one or more gods or spirits in charge of time.

It's your birthday!

Most people celebrate the day they were born, but this isn't the case everywhere. In Vietnam, it's rare to celebrate individual birth dates as everybody is considered to share the same birthday. Everyone becomes a year older after midnight on Tet – the Vietnamese holiday for New Year's Eve.

Gods of Time

In the Hindu religion, Shiva is both the creator and destroyer of time, while in Balinese mythology, Batara Kala is the god of time and destruction. Always hungry, he tries to eat the Sun and Moon, as well as unlucky people – charming! The Etruscans of ancient Italy commemorated their goddess of time, Nortia, by driving a long nail into a temple to mark each new year. The nail showed that the events of the previous year were now fixed and in the past.

Difficult Dates

In some cultures, certain dates are considered unlucky, such as Friday 13th in the UK, US and elsewhere. It's not certain how this superstition began, but the number 13 has long been thought to bring bad luck. In Norse myth, a dinner party of the gods was ruined by an uninvited guest called Loki, who made it 13 at the table and caused the world to be plunged into darkness.

8 AUGUST

For Hindus, the number 8 is linked with trouble and gloom, so the 8th day of the 8th month could be double trouble!

FRIDAY 17th

In Italy, 17 is thought to be unlucky because in Roman numerals it is XVII, an anagram of VIXI, Latin for 'my life is over'.

9 SEPTEMBER

The number 9 is unlucky in Japan, as when spoken it sounds like the Japanese word for pain.

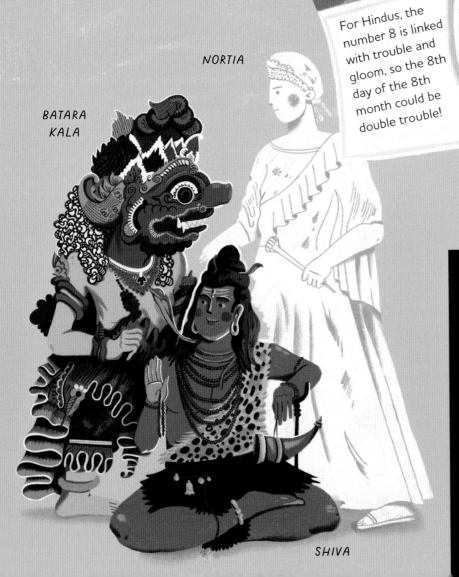

NORTIA

BATARA KALA

SHIVA

Ancient Astrology

The first known astrologers were the Babylonians, around 3,500 years ago. They believed that a person's fortunes on Earth were influenced by when they were born and the positions of the stars and planets.

In the Chinese zodiac, or Shengxiao, a person's fortune is decided by their year of birth. The zodiac is made up of 12-year cycles, with each year represented by an animal and certain personality traits. The order these animals appear in the zodiac is said to be their finishing order in a great race organised by the mythical Jade Emperor.

TIGER
2010
2022
Born leader, brave, intense, selfish

RABBIT
2011
2023
Popular, artistic, kind, timid

DRAGON
2012
2024
Outspoken, perfectionist, fearless, energetic

SNAKE
2013
2025
Calm, good at solving problems, aloof, jealous

OX
2009
2021
Patient, kind, reliable, stubborn

RAT
2008
2020
Quick-witted, ambitious, persuasive, critical of others

HORSE
2014
2026
Confident, enthusiastic, likes travel, bored by routine

PIG
2007
2019
Caring, tolerant, impatient, likes luxury

DOG
2006
2018
Patient, faithful, honest, sometimes anxious

ROOSTER
2005
2017
Independent, practical, hardworking, boastful

MONKEY
2016
2028
Fun, sociable, unpredictable

SHEEP (OR GOAT)
2015
2027
Easygoing, cheerful, disorganised

QUESTION TIME

Throughout history, people have held different views on what time is all about. Some think of it as travelling in circles, some in straight lines. Others wonder whether it is a property of the Universe like gravity, or is something we just imagine.

Illusion or Absolute?

Ibn Sīnā was a Muslim philosopher who thought that time was created by our memories and what we expect to happen.

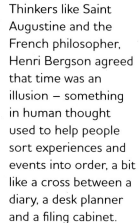

IBN SĪNĀ

Thinkers like Saint Augustine and the French philosopher, Henri Bergson agreed that time was an illusion – something in human thought used to help people sort experiences and events into order, a bit like a cross between a diary, a desk planner and a filing cabinet.

HENRI BERGSON

Lines or Circles?

The Ancient Greeks, some 2,500 years ago, were one of the first civilisations to really think about time. Many Greeks thought of it as a river that flowed from source to sea, meaning that time moved forwards in a straight line from the past to the future.

Other civilisations, including the Diné (Navajo), Hopi, Maya and Incas, developed the idea of time moving in circular cycles, which saw time repeat itself. Whatever people did, the seasons would come round again, the Sun would appear in the sky and crops would grow.

In Tibetan Buddhism, the bhāvacakra or 'wheel of life' describes how time travels in similar repeated circles of life, death and rebirth.

PART OF THE BUDDHIST BHĀVACAKRA SHOWING LIFE AS A CIRCLE OR WHEEL.

Forward or Back?

Many think of time as running in order from the past through the present towards the future. We say, we're 'looking forward' to something that will happen in the future and we 'look back' at something from the past.

The Aymara people who live in the Andes mountain range, think of time the other way round. They consider the future as unknown and unseen, and so it lurks behind them and isn't worth talking about as much as the past, which is known. As the past is so clearly remembered, it stands ahead of them.

In the Aymara language, spoken by more than 2 million people, 'qhipa' means 'back' or 'behind', and 'qhipa mara' means 'next year'.

Famous scientist Sir Isaac Newton disagreed. He believed in absolute time, and was convinced that time would exist even if the Universe was empty. To him, time is independent of other things and works the same way wherever you are in the Universe.

RENÉ DESCARTES

What is 'Now'?

We think of 'now' as the present but what does that mean?

French philosopher, René Descartes believed that 'now' is all there is, and that time is made up of a very long series of 'now' moments all strung together.

WILLIAM JAMES

Others, like Sir Isaac Newton, didn't think that now (the present) was a period of time at all. It was just the border between what has happened (the past) and what is about to happen (the future).

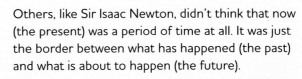
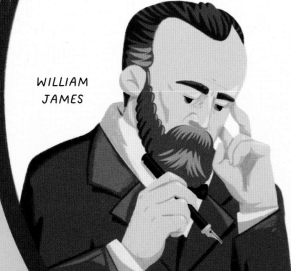

A third view was held by the American philosopher William James, who argued that now was a short period of time – he estimated 12 seconds – in which things appear to be happening in the present.

LIKE CLOCKWORK

Eight hundred years ago, most people had no need for time – they got up at dawn, spent the day farming and went to bed when it got dark. Fast forward 500 years in Europe, and clocks were everywhere! How did it happen?

BUILT IN 1410, THE ORLOJ CLOCK IN PRAGUE SHOWS THE TIME AND POSITION OF THE SUN IN THE SKY.

Look, No Hands

We get the word 'clock' from the Latin *clocca*, meaning 'bell'. The first mechanical clocks were invented in Europe over 700 years ago, but didn't have faces or hour and minute hands. Instead, they rang bells in church towers to summon people to pray at set times.

These early clocks worked using a heavy weight, which was winched up high in the air. As it slowly descended and unwound a rope or cable, it provided mechanical power to move the clock's parts. At set times, the clock mechanism would move metal hammers to strike bells. Because these early clocks needed plenty of height for the clock's weight to fall, they were mounted high up in towers.

Fancy Features

By the 15th century, clocks had gained faces and an hour hand. Some had minute hands, too, but they weren't that much use, as most early clocks could gain or lose an hour or more by the end of the day. Clocks by this time were becoming common in towns as well as churches, housed in town halls and clock towers. Some clocks were absolute beauties and entertained townsfolk with elaborate displays of moving mechanical figures including jousting knights, juggling jesters and moving stars and planets.

Spring Power

An alternative to falling weights came with the invention of the spring-powered clock in the 15th century. A metal spring called a mainspring was wound up tight by a key and then made to unwind very slowly, which powered the movement of the clock's parts. Mainsprings meant that clocks could be built much smaller. Now, people could keep clocks in their homes, and even wear them!

The first watches appeared around 500 years ago in Germany. They were worn around the neck or tucked into waistcoat pockets. Most men didn't wear a watch on their wrist until after World War One.

16TH-CENTURY WATCH

Changing Habits

Clocks eventually changed the way people lived. Before, there was no 10:45 or half past two. Clocks enabled time to be measured accurately and reliably. Suddenly, group activities could be organised at a precise moment.

When smaller clocks became affordable and entered many people's homes and businesses, it meant people were influenced by time... all the time! Shops, markets, banks and all sorts of other places began opening and closing at set times, not just sunrise and sunset. People became more conscious of time and now had a new standard they had to keep to – being punctual and on time.

Instead of relying on their own body clock (see p.60), people now ate or slept when the clock indicated a certain time of day, not when they felt hungry or sleepy.

When factories and industries grew in the 18th and 19th centuries, clocks proved vital in organising work. People found they were measured by time and punished if they were late or didn't do enough work in the hours. Some unscrupulous managers tampered with their clocks, making them run slow so they got more hours of work out of their employees for free!

32

ADVANCES IN TIME

As people's lives became more tied to time, the accuracy of clocks — or rather the lack of it — became a problem. Fortunately, a number of advances allowed clocks to keep time better.

Swing Time

Around 1602, Italian scientist Galileo Galilei found that pendulums (swinging weights hung from a fixed point) took the exact same amount of time to complete each of their swings. This handy fact was seized upon by Dutch scientist Christiaan Huygens, who used a pendulum to keep time in his new type of clock in 1656. At the end of a day, a pendulum clock might be out by only 15 seconds — a giant leap forward compared to the clocks that went before.

Pendulum Clocks

Here's how a pendulum clock works:

1. A weight falls slowly. As it falls, it turns the main wheel.

2. The main wheel turns the clock's hands. A set of gears allows the hour, minute and second hands to turn at different speeds.

3. To make sure the clock's hands turn accurately, the speed of the falling weight is controlled by the pendulum. As the pendulum swings, a mechanism called the anchor tilts back and forth. Each time it tilts, it lifts briefly off the escape wheel, allowing the wheel to turn very slightly. This creates the clock's tick-tocking sound.

4. Winding the clock turns the main wheel anticlockwise and raises the weight back up again. This is normally done every day or two.

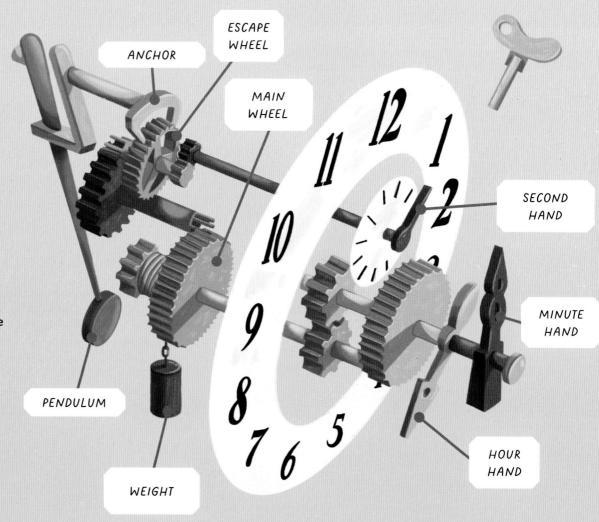

ANCHOR

ESCAPE WHEEL

MAIN WHEEL

SECOND HAND

MINUTE HAND

HOUR HAND

PENDULUM

WEIGHT

Crystal Clocks

The pendulum clock remained king until the 20th century, when a new type of clock was invented: the quartz clock. Scientists found that when electricity was passed through a small piece of quartz crystal, the crystal oscillates (vibrates back and forth) at a precise rate: 32,768 times a second. When the crystal was placed in an electric circuit that could count these vibrations, time could be displayed by the quartz clock very accurately. These quartz clocks (and, later, quartz watches) were accurate to half a second or less per day. Brilliant!

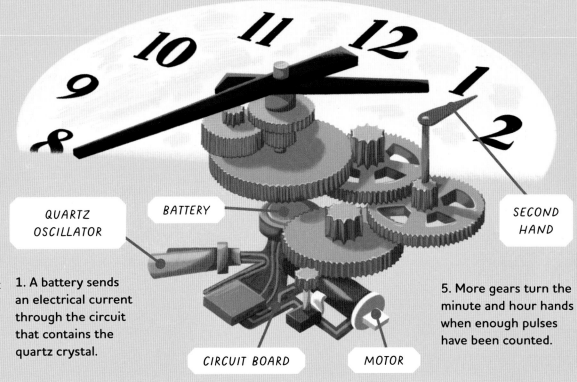

QUARTZ OSCILLATOR

BATTERY

SECOND HAND

CIRCUIT BOARD

MOTOR

1. A battery sends an electrical current through the circuit that contains the quartz crystal.

2. The crystal vibrates at 32,768 vibrations per second.

3. The circuit counts the vibrations and sends a single electrical pulse after every second.

4. The pulses power a tiny electric motor that turns the clock's gears, moving the second hand.

5. More gears turn the minute and hour hands when enough pulses have been counted.

Atomic Clocks

Quartz clocks were the last word in accuracy for a mere 25 years or so before the arrival of the ultimate in timekeeping. Atomic clocks count the vibrations of atoms such as caesium 133, which can move back and forth 9,192,631,770 times per second. After years of work, they've proven to be incredibly accurate and reliable.

Everything from world time zones to GPS now relies on atomic time. A network of more than 260 atomic clocks positioned all over the planet supply the world with super accurate time. Some watches and clocks today use radio signals to get their time direct from this network of atomic clocks.

The JILA Quantum Gas atomic clock in the US is accurate to +/- 1/10th second every 14 billion years – just over the lifetime of the Universe!

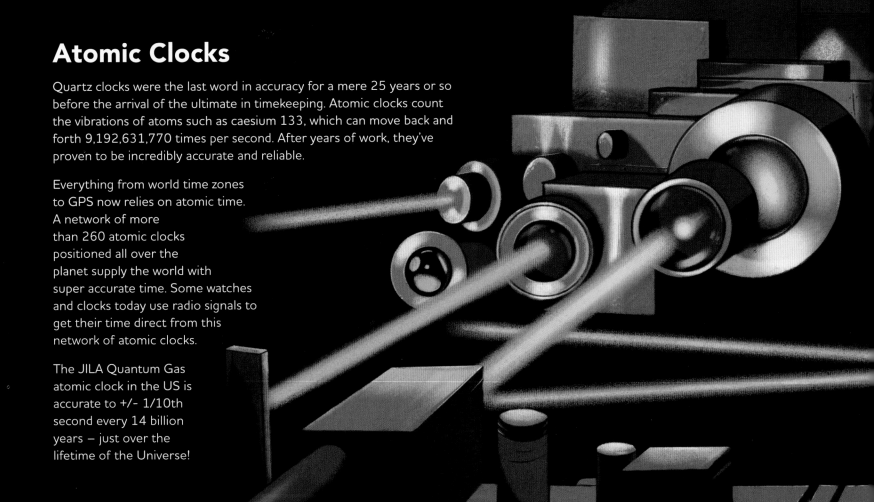

CHAMPION CLOCKS

Clocks are sometimes more than just a way of telling the time. They can become a local landmark and visitor attraction, drawing tourists to view them. Some have become celebrities in their own right!

Big Ben

Housed in Elizabeth Tower, part of London's Palace of Westminster, is a famous clock with four faces. Everyone knows it as Big Ben, which is the name of the giant 13.7-tonne bell the clock strikes. The clock takes over an hour to wind up and keeps time by swinging a 4.4-m-long pendulum, which weighs 310 kg – the weight of five people. Adding or removing an old English penny coin to the pendulum's mechanism alters the clock's speed by 0.4 seconds per day.

Knit-Tock

Norwegian artist Siren Elise Wilhelmsen built a clock that measures time in terms of how much knitting it does! Her clock knits a precisely 2-m-long scarf in 365 days. The clock has been exhibited in museums all across the world.

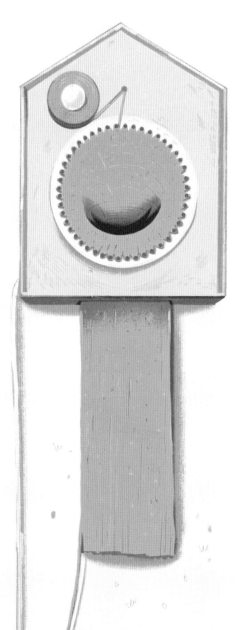

The Augenroller (Eye Roller)

The Augenroller clock in Koblenz, Germany features a sculpture of the face of a robber beheaded in the 16th century. As the clock's pendulum moves, the face rolls its eyes and sticks out its tongue every 30 minutes.

Cuckoo Clock

The world's largest cuckoo clock is found in Triberg-Schonach in Germany and looks like an entire house. It is 60 times bigger than a regular cuckoo clock. The bird that pops out on the hour and half hour is 4.5 m long and weighs 150 kg.

Rathaus Glockenspiel

This complicated clock in Munich, Germany, puts on a play set to music at 11am and noon every day. The scene lasts 12 or 15 minutes and involves 32 mechanical figures including jousting knights and dancing barrel makers.

31 Hands

The Vacheron Constantin Reference 57260 is the world's most complicated watch. It contains 2,826 parts and features time zones, alarms, a moving star chart and 31 hands. It took 8 years to design and build and was sold for around US$10 million.

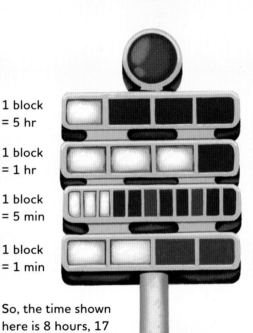

1 block = 5 hr

1 block = 1 hr

1 block = 5 min

1 block = 1 min

So, the time shown here is 8 hours, 17 minutes or 08:17.

Makkah Clock Tower

Found in Mecca, Saudi Arabia, this four-sided clock is the tallest and largest in the world. The centre of each clock is a dizzying 430 m above the ground, and each clock face is a gigantic 43 m wide – six times bigger than Big Ben's – and features a 23-m-long minute hand. It takes over 2,000,000 LED lights to illuminate the faces at night.

Water Clock

There's a very unusual water clock at Osaka Station in Japan. A computer controls patterns of falling water droplets from a long row of nozzles. The water forms a 6.5-m-wide digital clock display.

Mengenlehreuhr

The unusual Mengenlehreuhr clock in Berlin, Germany, represents the time as a series of coloured lights. Each of the lit-up blocks represents a certain period of time.

ALARMING STORIES

Today, if we need to wake up at a certain time we can set an alarm on a clock or a phone. But what did people do in the past?

Time to Get Up

Many people used natural cues like birdsong or the Sun streaming into their bedroom to get up and start their day. Others were woken by the chiming of church bells or crowing of a rooster.

In the 19th century, many workers lived in housing beside the factory they worked in. Factory owners built powerful whistles that signalled it was time to get up and put in a shift of work.

Knocker Uppers

Before alarm clocks were common, people who needed to get up earlier for work than others in their household often paid a subscription to a knocker-upper service. These employed people to wander around town armed with long bamboo poles, which they used to tap on an upstairs bedroom window to wake up their client. Common in factory towns with 4am work starts, there were still a handful of knocker uppers at work in the 1950s in England.

Sound the Alarm

The first bedside alarm clock we know of was built by a young American clockmaker called Levi Hutchins in 1787. It could only sound an alarm (ringing a small bell) at one fixed time, 4am. This was the time Hutchins liked to wake up every day of the year! Adjustable mechanical alarm clocks didn't arrive for another 70 years. French and German clockmakers produced small clocks that used a hammer to strike one or two metal bells, creating quite a din.

Instead of lugging a really long pole around, one ingenious knocker upper in London called Mary Smith used a peashooter to fire dried peas at the windows.

In 1891, the Early Riser's Friend appeared – it was the world's first attempt at a 'teasmade', a device that makes a hot drink at the time its alarm goes off.

Strange Alarm Clocks

Over the years, designers have dreamt up lots of inventive ways to wake people up – and stop them falling back asleep again!

In 1867, a mechanical bed went on sale in Paris. When its alarm clock rang, gears whirred and turned and the bed tilted to tip the person out. An eccentric British writer called William Strachey bought the bed and rigged it out so it would tip him out straight into his bath.

Some alarm clocks are designed to get you up and out of bed so you are in less danger of hitting the snooze button. There are wheeled alarm clocks that whizz around the room and even flying alarm clocks with detachable parts that you need to catch before the alarm will stop!

Some alarm clocks wake you up much more gently, with music or pleasant, natural smells. Sunrise alarm clocks take the alarm clock story all the way back to the beginning, by turning on lamps that simulate the changing intensity and colours of the rising Sun.

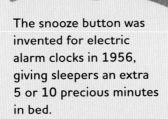

The snooze button was invented for electric alarm clocks in 1956, giving sleepers an extra 5 or 10 precious minutes in bed.

TIME TO EXPLORE

The 16th and 17th centuries were boom time for explorers from Europe. Seafarers set off on epic voyages across uncharted oceans, wondering what they would encounter. There was one big problem though: how could sailors in the middle of the ocean know exactly where they were?

Dead Reckoning

Early sailors sailed close to shore so they could use coastal landmarks to navigate. When they did have to sail through uncharted waters they used something called dead reckoning. They measured the time using hourglasses and gauged the speed they were sailing at to work out the distance they'd travelled.

In 1707, four British Royal Navy ships sailed off course and were wrecked on the rocky coasts of the Scilly Islands, causing the loss of more than 1,400 lives.

The Longitude Problem

The trouble with dead reckoning is that tiny errors in measurement easily build up, especially in unknown, featureless oceans. To get a precise measurement of their location, sailors needed to know their ship's latitude and longitude (see box, opposite).

A rough idea of latitude could be found by measuring the angle of the Sun above the horizon. At noon each day (with the Sun at its highest), sailors used a device called an astrolabe to take readings, before converting this figure into latitude using a printed table.

Longitude wasn't so easy to calculate. It needed really accurate clocks on ships, but the best available timepieces, pendulum clocks, were no good at sea. The rocking of the ship interfered with the swinging of their pendulum, making them wildly inaccurate — out by more than an hour each day. As a result, sailors resorted to guessing their longitude, which sometimes ended with their ships wrecked.

What are Latitude and Longitude?

Latitude and longitude are imaginary lines that circle the planet.

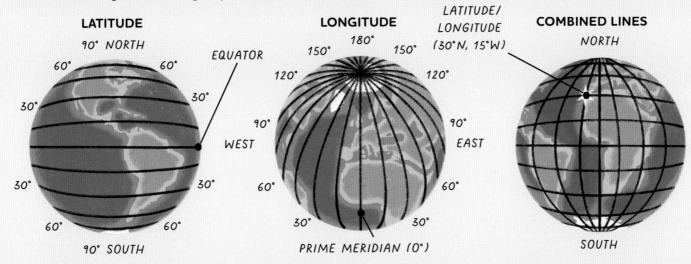

LATITUDE

90° NORTH
60°   60°
30°   30°
EQUATOR
WEST
30°   30°
60°   60°
90° SOUTH

LONGITUDE

180°
150°   150°
120°   120°
90°   90°
WEST   EAST
60°   60°
30°   30°
PRIME MERIDIAN (0°)

LATITUDE/ LONGITUDE (30°N, 15°W)

COMBINED LINES

NORTH

SOUTH

LATITUDE lines are used to calculate how far north or south of the equator you are. The 0° line is the equator, 90° N is the North Pole and 90° S, the South Pole.

LONGITUDE lines travel from the North Pole to the South Pole. They divide Earth up into segments that run from 180° E to 180° W. These show how far east or west you are of the Prime Meridian line (0°), which runs through London, UK.

If you know your latitude and your longitude then you can plot these coordinates on a map and know precisely where you are.

The Longitude Solution

From the 1500s onwards, major naval nations like Spain, Portugal and Britain offered handsome rewards for a solution. The problem occupied the minds of famous scientists like Christiaan Huygens and Sir Isaac Newton, all without success.

In 1714, the British government offered up to £20,000 (equal to many millions today) to anyone who could solve the problem. English carpenter and clockmaker John Harrison (1693–1776) devoted much of his life to scooping the prize, which he finally achieved in his seventies. He built a series of accurate, mechanical clocks called marine chronometers. Instead of pendulums, these clocks contained incredibly intricate balances and gearing that could withstand the damp, extremes of temperatures and constant swaying to and fro that occurred at sea. These accurate clocks finally made it possible for sailors to calculate longitude at sea.

Harrison's H4 chronometer was his masterpiece. This 13-cm-wide, handheld watch proved extremely accurate on two test voyages across the Atlantic – to within one-fifth of a second a day.

HIGH TIME

Time's amazing ability to tell us where we are on our planet has entered the space age thanks to satellites orbiting high above Earth. There are a number of satellite navigation systems, including Russia's GLONASS, Japan's QZSS and China's BeiDou. But the most famous of all is the US-run Global Positioning System, or GPS.

How Does it Work?

Currently, the GPS system is made up of 31 NAVSTAR satellites orbiting Earth, 20,200 km above its surface. Twenty-four are in use at any one time, arranged in groups of four, each following the same orbit. They circle the planet twice a day and make sure that four satellites are viewable at any one time from almost any point on Earth.

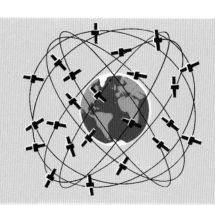

1. Each satellite is equipped with a number of super-accurate and expensive atomic clocks (see p.33). These keep track of time to within 3 billionths of a second.

2. Many times each second, the time and the satellite's precise position is sent as a signal back to Earth using radio waves.

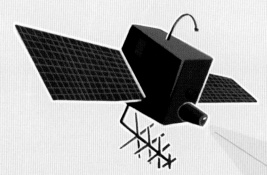

3. A GPS receiver on Earth gathers in signals from four satellites. It compares the time taken to receive each signal to calculate its distance from each of them. From that data, it can then know its location on Earth to within mere metres.

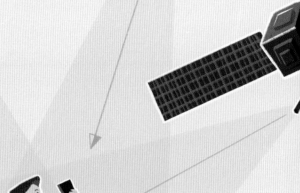

Every Split-Second Counts

GPS signals travel at the speed of light, meaning they race along around 30 cm every billionth of a second. If the timekeeping on GPS satellites drifts or is not perfectly in sync, the system can no longer navigate accurately.

An accurate GPS system can pinpoint your position to within 3–6 m.

Being just a millionth of a second out of sync means accuracy can drop 300 m or more.

A thousandth of a second out, could make GPS accurate only to 300 km. So a GPS receiver might not be able to tell whether you were in London or Paris!

Amazing Applications

GPS was originally used just by military forces but now it's available to everyone. It's used to power car satellite navigation systems and to give runners, walkers and cyclists information about their time, speed and distance. It's also used for a surprisingly wide range of other applications.

Fitting endangered animals with a GPS transmitter allows naturalists to track them and helps protect them from poachers.

Slim GPS trackers attached to artworks can trace their whereabouts if they are stolen.

Guided by GPS, driverless tractors can plough and prepare farm fields, leaving farmers to perform other work.

GPS receivers mounted on floating buoys out at sea help track the size and spread of oil slicks and other chemical spills.

Helicopters use GPS to map the edges of forest wildfires to alert firefighters on the ground.

Some artists have fitted GPS trackers to their bicycles to create art out of their cycle routes in map programs.

IN THE ZONE

If you travel a long distance east or west, chances are you will have to change the time on your watch. This is because your destination operates in a different time zone to your home. How did time zones come about?

How Zones Work

The world is divided into 24 time zones by lines running from the North Pole to the South Pole called meridians. Each zone spans 15 degrees of Earth's 360 degrees. The time zones east of the Prime Meridian line are ahead of Greenwich Mean Time (GMT), while the time zones to the west are behind it.

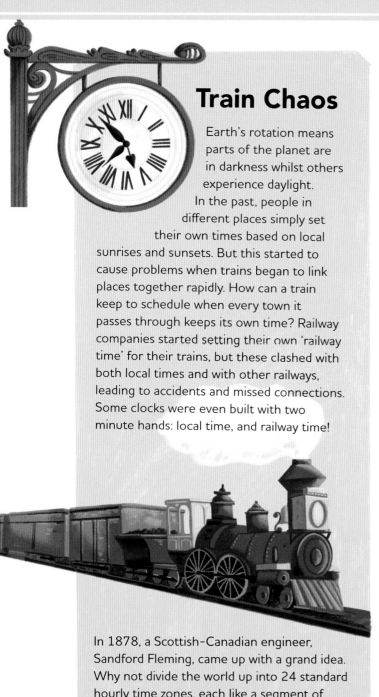

Train Chaos

Earth's rotation means parts of the planet are in darkness whilst others experience daylight. In the past, people in different places simply set their own times based on local sunrises and sunsets. But this started to cause problems when trains began to link places together rapidly. How can a train keep to schedule when every town it passes through keeps its own time? Railway companies started setting their own 'railway time' for their trains, but these clashed with both local times and with other railways, leading to accidents and missed connections. Some clocks were even built with two minute hands: local time, and railway time!

In 1878, a Scottish-Canadian engineer, Sandford Fleming, came up with a grand idea. Why not divide the world up into 24 standard hourly time zones, each like a segment of an orange? A conference in 1884 agreed, and made Greenwich Mean Time (GMT) the starting point. GMT is the time measured on the Prime Meridian line (see p.39), which passes through the Royal Greenwich Observatory in London.

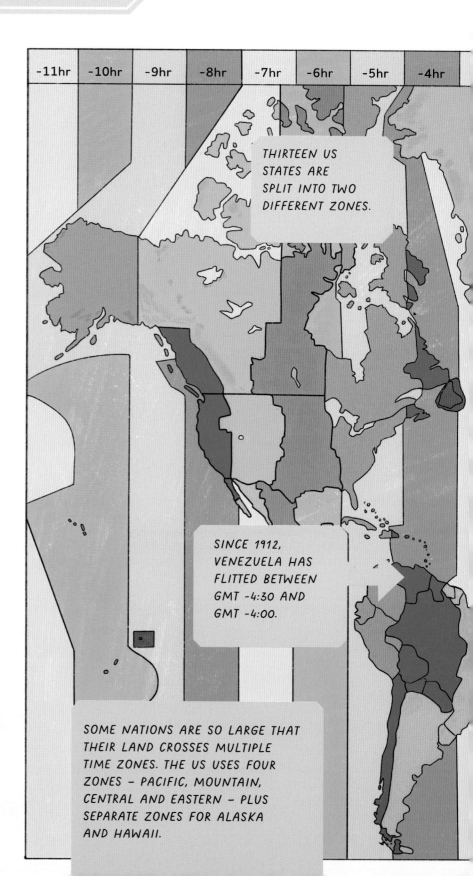

-11hr -10hr -9hr -8hr -7hr -6hr -5hr -4hr

THIRTEEN US STATES ARE SPLIT INTO TWO DIFFERENT ZONES.

SINCE 1912, VENEZUELA HAS FLITTED BETWEEN GMT -4:30 AND GMT -4:00.

SOME NATIONS ARE SO LARGE THAT THEIR LAND CROSSES MULTIPLE TIME ZONES. THE US USES FOUR ZONES - PACIFIC, MOUNTAIN, CENTRAL AND EASTERN - PLUS SEPARATE ZONES FOR ALASKA AND HAWAII.

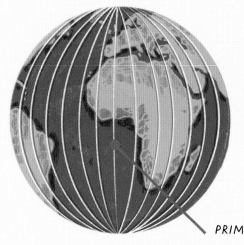

If you're in London at midday and phone someone in Asia who might be in the GMT +5 time zone, it will be 5pm – 5 hours ahead of you. Making another noon call to someone in the GMT -8 time zone is likely to annoy them as you'll be waking them up at 4am in the morning!

An International Date

The International Date Line is halfway round the world from the Prime Meridian line. It runs through the middle of the Pacific Ocean and marks the end of one day and the start of another. Crossing the line sees you lose or gain a day.

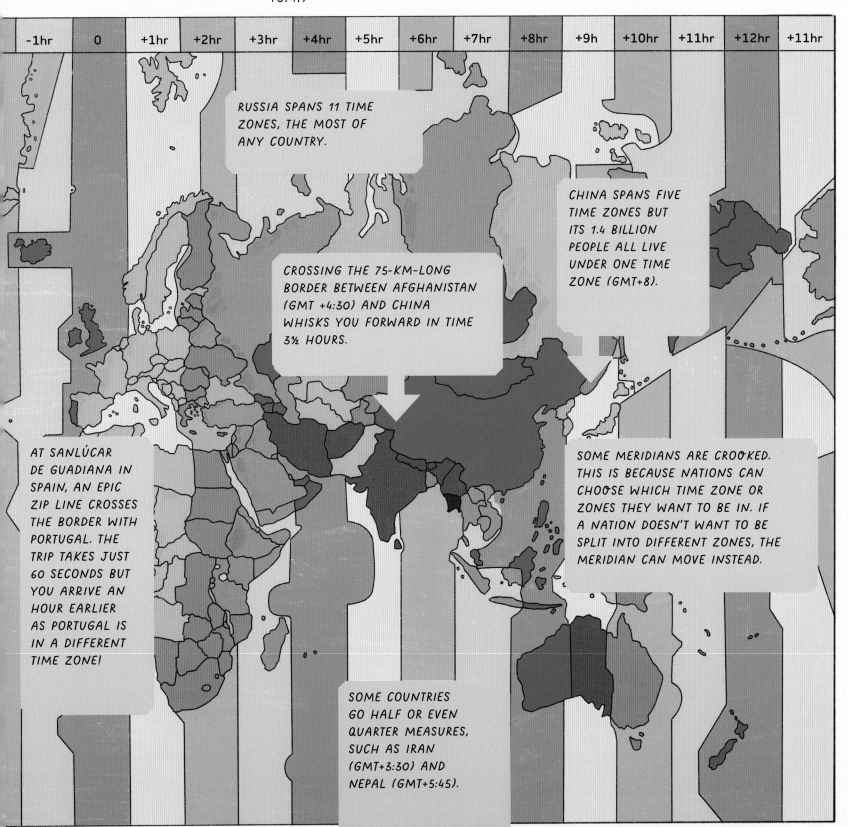

SAVING THE DAY

Almost half the world tinkers with time every spring and autumn. Daylight saving time (DST) sees the clocks turned forward 1 hour in spring to create an extra hour of daylight in the evening during late spring and summer. That lost hour of sleep annoys some, but the extra light is enjoyed by many.

Free For All

After World War Two, any US city or region could choose to go for daylight saving time or not and pick the dates when it applied. This led to chaos for transport companies with strict schedules. Some bus routes required passengers to reset their watches six or seven times during their 50-minute journey! The US passed a law in 1966 insisting places made changes on the same two dates in spring and autumn. In 2007, the autumn date was pushed back to the first Sunday in November so it wasn't so dark for kids playing trick or treat on Halloween. Boo!

Spring Forward, Fall Back

In the UK, the clocks go forward 1 hour at 1am on the last Sunday in March, and back 1 hour at 2am on the last Sunday in October. Other countries alter their clocks on different dates or hours, but all do it at night when fewer people are awake. Some, like Syria and Paraguay, make the change at midnight. This means when the clocks go back in autumn you travel back to 11pm the previous day!

Seize The Light

The first countries to adopt daylight saving were Germany and Austria in 1916. They were in the middle of World War One and thought the extra hour of light in the evening would save lots of energy, which could be used to power the war effort. The countries they were fighting quickly adopted it as well. In the US, it was known as Fast Time whilst in the UK, it was called British Summer Time. When World War Two came around, the Brits doubled up, adding on two hours each spring from 1941 to 1945.

SAVING DAYLIGHT!

"SET THE CLOCK AHEAD ONE HOUR AND WIN THE WAR"

MOBILIZE AN EXTRA HOUR OF DAYLIGHT AND HELP WIN THE WAR!

STOP A STOP B STOP C STOP D

Time Twins

In 2016, Emily Peterson gave birth to unusual twin boys in Cape Cod Hospital in the US. Samuel was born first but his twin brother, Ronan is officially the oldest! The reason? Samuel was born at 1:39am, just before the clocks went back an hour. Although Ronan arrived 31 minutes later, daylight saving meant his time of birth was given as 1:10am, making him the oldest.

Where in the World?

At present, around 70 countries use daylight saving time. Most countries near the equator don't bother as they get pretty much the same amount of daylight all year round. Elsewhere, some countries really can't make up their mind. Since 1916, Portugal has adopted or dropped DST 13 times and Turkey 16 times!

STRANGE TIMES

Some strange things have happened to time over the years. It has been bought and sold, taxed and tinkered with, and measured and named in odd ways.

Tax on Time

In 1797, the British government introduced a new tax... on clocks and watches. Anyone owning a gold or silver watch or clock had to pay 10 shillings — equal to about £65 today! The tax proved wildly unpopular, especially with clockmakers, hundreds of whom were put out of work. The tax was removed the following year.

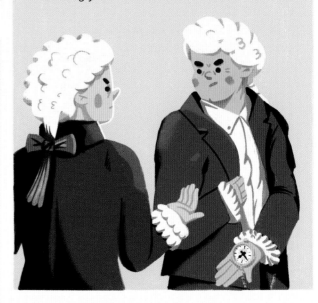

Selling Time

Before radio and other forms of telecommunications, it wasn't easy for people to keep accurate time. Most watches and clocks of the 19th century needed to be corrected frequently — but how did people know what time to reset their timepieces to?

One member of staff at the Royal Observatory in Greenwich, John Belville, had a business-savvy idea. John's family had a chronometer pocket watch, which was accurate to within 1/10th of a second per day. Every morning, John set the watch to the time of the Royal Observatory's clock, then travelled through London selling the time to people by letting them look at his watch. It sounds unlikely, but his service was a big success. His wife and his daughter, Ruth, also sold people the time, both working into their eighties. The business lasted from 1836 to 1940.

Worm Day

Into the 20th century, the people living in the Trobriand Islands, off the coast of New Guinea in Asia, had a very strange starting point for their new year. It began on Worm Day every October. This was when swarms of palolo worms appeared from the sea to lay their eggs.

All About Me

In 2002, the president of Turkmenistan, Saparmurat Niyazov, renamed all the months of the year. September was renamed Ruhnama after a book of poems the president had written, and April was renamed Gurbansoltan after his mother! The new names were used until 2008.

On an Internet Time watch, 41.6 .beats equal a regular hour.

.BEATS TIME

@860
20:38

LOCAL TIME
IN GMT+1
TIME ZONE

Beat the Clock

In 1998, Swiss watchmaker Swatch tried to introduce decimal time again, 200 years after the French had failed. Its 'Internet Time' watches and clocks featured days divided into 1,000 decimal minutes called 'beats' with each .beat lasting 86.4 regular seconds. It didn't catch on.

Time Revolution

In 1793, France changed its calendar, making each week 10 days long and each month 3 weeks long. More dramatically, it changed its clocks to French Revolutionary Time. This consisted of just 10 hours, not 24, with each hour containing 100 minutes and each minute made up of 100 seconds.

The experiment proved confusing and expensive (every clock in the country had to be replaced) and began to be abandoned 2 years later. But the new weeks and months of the year lasted until 1806.

Under the decimal system, 1:30am was 0:62, noon was 5:00, and 3pm was 6:25.

No More Weekends

Imagine losing your weekends for over 11 years. That was what happened to people living in the Soviet Union in 1929. Their ruler, Josef Stalin, created a *nepreryvka* or continuous working week. It was 5 days long and workers were randomly granted 1 day in 5 off, even if the rest of their family still had to work. Holiday plans were ruined! Stalin changed the week to 6 days the following year, but weekends didn't return until 1940.

1929

1940

THE WORLD OVER TIME

Humans tend to focus on short periods of time, but the planet operates on far longer timescales. How does Earth change over time, and how long does it take for features to emerge or transform?

Mountain Building

Dinosaurs never got to see the Himalayas. Shame. Earth's highest mountain range didn't exist when dinosaurs lived, 66–245 million years ago. In fact, 100 million years ago, India was an island situated south of the equator. As it moved northwards, it crushed up against Asia and thrust huge amounts of rock upwards, some of which formed the Himalayas. The process is still occuring. This means the highest mountain on Earth, Mount Everest, is growing 0.5–1 cm taller every year.

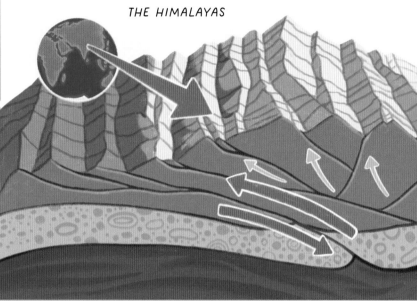

THE HIMALAYAS

Shifting Continents

Earth's crust is made up of a number of gigantic tectonic plates. These fit together a little like a jigsaw, but can move apart or under one another in a process called continental drift. The rate of drift may not sound much – just 1–8 cm a year – but over time, this has seen some astonishing changes.

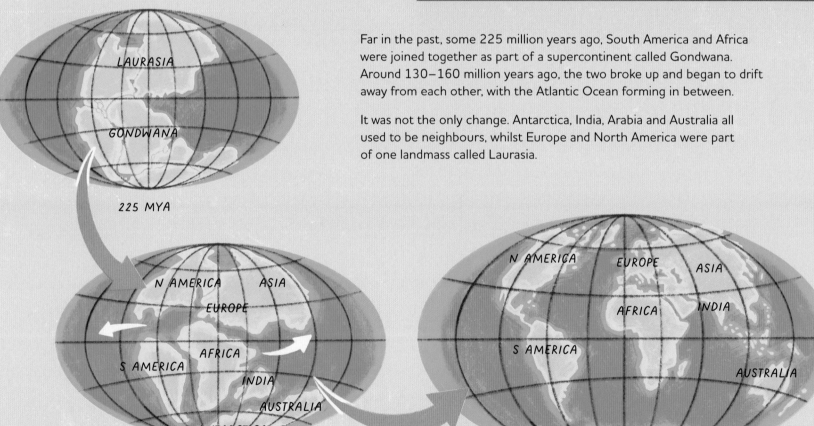

225 MYA

100 MYA

TODAY

Far in the past, some 225 million years ago, South America and Africa were joined together as part of a supercontinent called Gondwana. Around 130–160 million years ago, the two broke up and began to drift away from each other, with the Atlantic Ocean forming in between.

It was not the only change. Antarctica, India, Arabia and Australia all used to be neighbours, whilst Europe and North America were part of one landmass called Laurasia.

Shaping the Landscape

Other processes also shape the landscape over time. Erosion is the wearing away of rock by natural forces like wind or water. Rivers can cut into and completely transform a landscape. In the case of the Colorado River in the US, it created something rather wonderful: the 448-km-long, 1.8-km-deep Grand Canyon, which it sculpted over 5–6 million years.

Volcanoes

Volcanoes usually form over thousands of years from activity underground and eruptions on the surface. But occasionally, a volcano can form in double-quick time. On 20th February, 1943, an eruption in a cornfield began in Paricutin, Mexico. Within 24 hours, a 50-m-high cone had appeared! By the end of the week it was 150 m high. Today it stands 424 m tall.

Growing Numbers

The human population has greatly increased over time, but not at a constant rate. In 10,000 BCE, there may have been just 4 million people on the planet, fewer than live in the city of Montreal in Canada. Today, the population is increasing by approximately 1 billion people every 12 years – that's just over the population of Germany every year.

2022
8 billion

2000
6 billion

1985
Global population doubles to 4.87 billion in just 40 years.

1700
Population growth starts exploding.

1945
Humans total 2.4 billion.

3000 BCE
As ancient Egypt starts flourishing, around 45 million people exist worldwide.

1000 CE
About 323 million exist – fewer than the population of the US today.

1835
Population doubles between 1700 and 1835, to over a billion.

0 CE
Around 230–240 million people live on the planet.

3000 BCE | 0 CE | 1000 CE | 1700 | 1835 | 1945 | 1985

GEOLOGICAL TIME

Time on Earth began with our planet beginning to form around 4.54 billion years ago. Geological time describes Earth's long history in terms of its rocks. It is based on how layers of rock, known as strata, form, with the newest layers tending to be near the top and the oldest at the bottom.

Rock Stars

Geologists (rock scientists) use geological time to date fossils – the remains of once-living things – by what rock layer they appear in. They can narrow down dates for a fossil find by studying the layers immediately above and below the layer it was found in. The principle of 'superposition' means that a fossil in one layer is always younger than fossils found in rock layers beneath it. In other words, the deeper you dig, the farther back in time you go.

Index Fossils

As knowledge of fossils and rocks has grown, scientists can use a known fossil that lived within a narrow time period (called an 'index fossil') to date other mystery fossils and whole rock layers. For instance, a fossil found in the same layer as a T. Rex skeleton is likely to be from around 68–66 million years ago.

Time scale

The geological time scale is split up into what looks, at first glance, like a really confusing range of smaller and smaller units of time. But it's actually not that complicated.

FEARSOME TYRANNOSAURUS REX EXISTED 68–66 MILLION YEARS AGO (MYA)

PERISPHINCTES AMMONITE LIVED BETWEEN 201 AND 145 MYA

TRILOBITES EXISTED 521–221 MYA

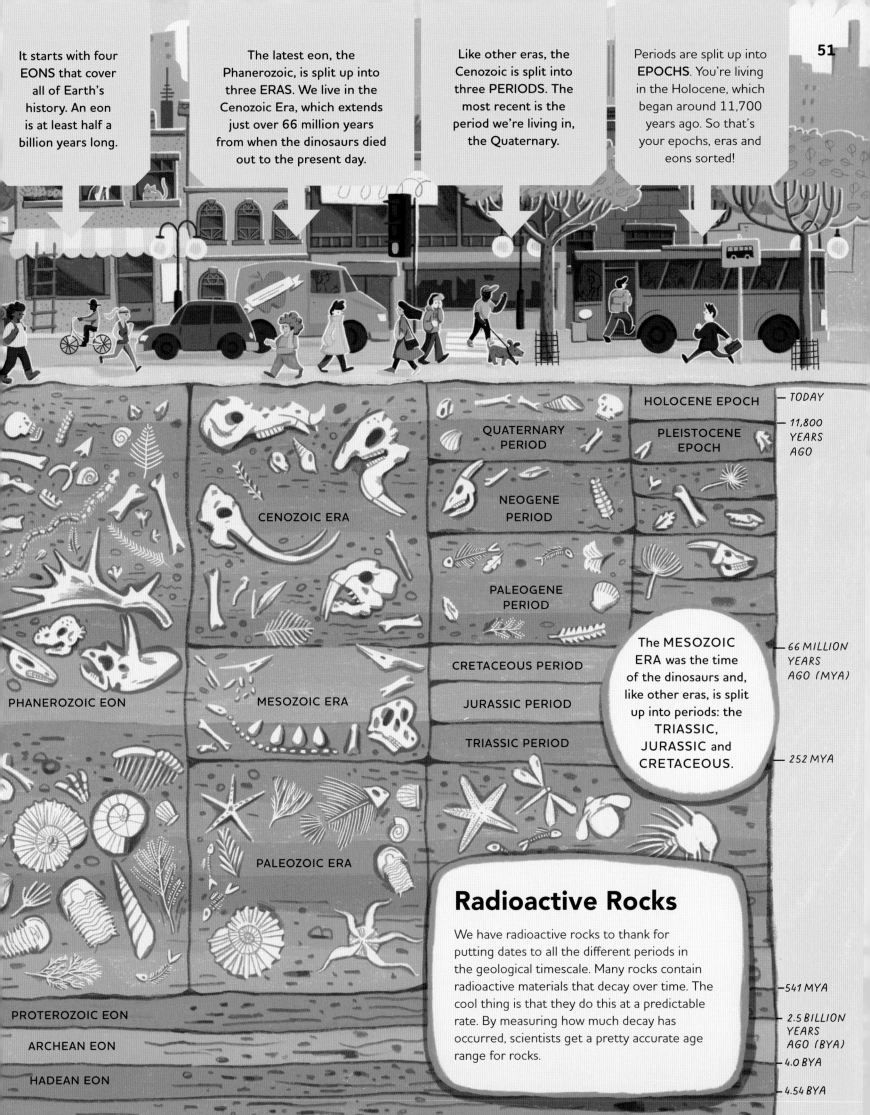

It starts with four EONS that cover all of Earth's history. An eon is at least half a billion years long.

The latest eon, the Phanerozoic, is split up into three ERAS. We live in the Cenozoic Era, which extends just over 66 million years from when the dinosaurs died out to the present day.

Like other eras, the Cenozoic is split into three PERIODS. The most recent is the period we're living in, the Quaternary.

Periods are split up into EPOCHS. You're living in the Holocene, which began around 11,700 years ago. So that's your epochs, eras and eons sorted!

HOLOCENE EPOCH — TODAY

QUATERNARY PERIOD

— 11,800 YEARS AGO

PLEISTOCENE EPOCH

CENOZOIC ERA

NEOGENE PERIOD

PALEOGENE PERIOD

The MESOZOIC ERA was the time of the dinosaurs and, like other eras, is split up into periods: the TRIASSIC, JURASSIC and CRETACEOUS.

— 66 MILLION YEARS AGO (MYA)

CRETACEOUS PERIOD

PHANEROZOIC EON

MESOZOIC ERA

JURASSIC PERIOD

— 252 MYA

TRIASSIC PERIOD

PALEOZOIC ERA

Radioactive Rocks

We have radioactive rocks to thank for putting dates to all the different periods in the geological timescale. Many rocks contain radioactive materials that decay over time. The cool thing is that they do this at a predictable rate. By measuring how much decay has occurred, scientists get a pretty accurate age range for rocks.

— 541 MYA

PROTEROZOIC EON

— 2.5 BILLION YEARS AGO (BYA)

ARCHEAN EON

— 4.0 BYA

HADEAN EON

— 4.54 BYA

HOW OLD?

How do we estimate the age of things older than ourselves, or date events long in the past? Well, science has found some pretty funky ways of telling the time when it comes to dating things.

Tree Rings

Every year, trees add a little extra growth to their trunk. They form a new outer ring just beneath their bark. The science of dendrochronology counts these rings to discover a tree's age, and more. Trees grow faster in years with more rain and also record signs of scarring from forest fires. This helps scientists build up a real picture of a tree's life.

Obviously, chopping a tree down to get a complete cross-section through a trunk kills the tree. So instead, scientists often take a small 'core sample' by boring all the way to the centre of a trunk and studying the small parts of the rings contained in the sample.

RAINY YEAR OR SEASON (WIDE RING)

OLDEST RINGS ARE NEARER THE CENTRE

SCARRING FROM FIRE

BARK

DRY YEAR (THIN RINGS)

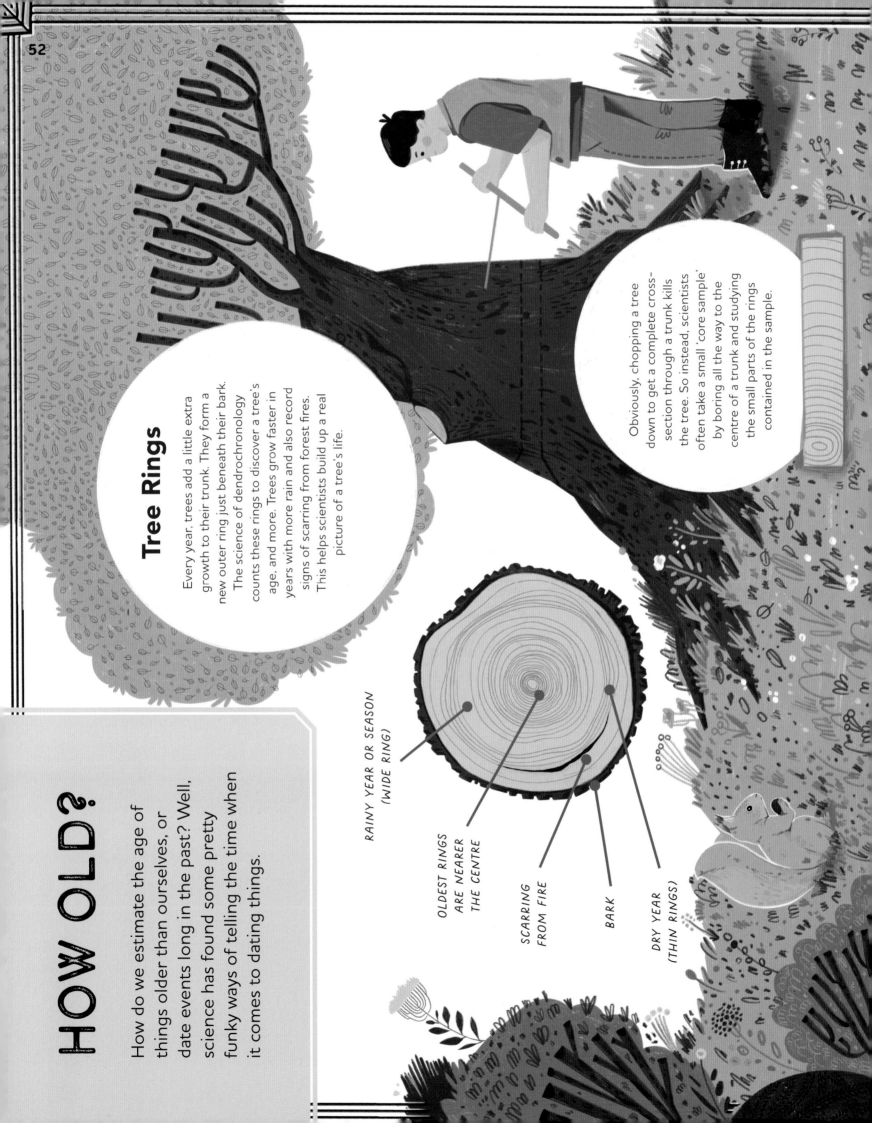

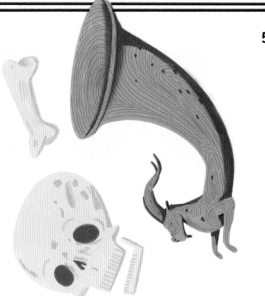

Growth Rings

Growth layers, or rings called circuli, build up each year on a bony fish's fin spines and in tiny stones in their ear called otoliths. Scientists can count these layers, a little like counting tree rings, to work out the fish's age. In sharks, similar growth rings occur on their vertebrae (backbone parts) each year.

Ice Cores

An ice core is a long, narrow cylinder obtained by drilling deep into glaciers or ice caps. These cores contain layer upon layer of snowfall that have built up over thousands of years and been compressed into ice. As the snow fell it carried dissolved chemicals and particles from the atmosphere, and these became part of the ice along with little bubbles of trapped air. This makes an ice core a brilliant record of conditions in the atmosphere many centuries ago.

OBTAINING AN ICE CORE IS A LITTLE LIKE CORING AN APPLE

Radiocarbon Dating

All living things absorb carbon from their food and the air around them. Some of this is carbon-14, a type of carbon that is radioactive and decays. When a plant or animal dies, it stops absorbing carbon, but the carbon-14 it contains continues to decay.

Scientists know how long it takes for half of the remaining carbon-14 to disappear. This is called its half-life and it's around 5,730 years. Because carbon-14 disappears at a steady rate, scientists can get a pretty good idea of how old a once-living thing is by measuring how much carbon-14 is left in it.

This technique has been used on old skeletons and artefacts made of materials like wood and leather. Radiocarbon dating has also helped prove that seemingly ancient artworks were in fact modern fakes.

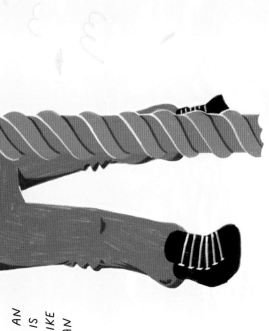

LIFESPANS

The length of time something lives or lasts is called its lifespan. Some materials, like plastic, last seemingly forever. Others, like a paper towel, rot away in a matter of weeks. In the natural world, living things age at wildly different rates. Some live for less than a year, others for centuries.

24 hours
An adult mayfly lives for 24 hours or less, a life so short that it doesn't even have a mouth to eat with.

42 days
This is the typical lifespan of Mouse-ear cress (*Arabidopsis thaliana*).

17 years
A standard ballpoint pen, if used to sign your signature once a day, will last this length of time.

5–7 days
Tiny gastrotrichs, under 1 mm long, live in sand and water. They go from an egg to an adult in 3 days and their entire lives are over in typically less than a week.

60 days
Found in coral reefs, the dwarf pygmy goby lives just 2 months.

14 years
The typical lifespan of the majestic tiger is surprisingly short. The average is lowered because many tigers die at a young age.

50–70 years
The typical lifespan of willow trees.

Less than 1 year
Annual flowering plants complete their lifecycle – from seed to mature plant to dying off – all in under 12 months.

12 years
The average lifespan of a typical modern washing machine.

2 years
This is the maximum age most weasels will reach, one of the shortest lifespans of any mammal.

Ancient albatross

Albatrosses normally live to a maximum of 40 years. In 2021, a female albatross at the Midway Atoll national wildlife refuge, in the Pacific Ocean, surprised wardens when she became a new mum at the age of 70!

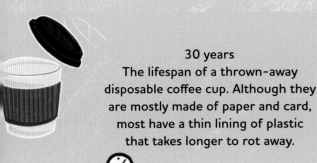

30 years
The lifespan of a thrown-away disposable coffee cup. Although they are mostly made of paper and card, most have a thin lining of plastic that takes longer to rot away.

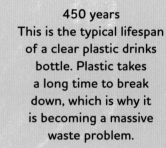

272+ years
A 5.6 m-long Greenland shark was studied in 2016 and thought to be between 272 and 512 years old.

40–60 years
Elephants, like many big mammals, have long lifespans.

225 years
Launched in 1797, the USS *Constitution* is the oldest ship still afloat.

450 years
This is the typical lifespan of a clear plastic drinks bottle. Plastic takes a long time to break down, which is why it is becoming a massive waste problem.

Oldest land animal

Jonathan, a giant Seychelles tortoise, celebrated his 190th birthday in 2022. Scientists estimate that he was about 50 years old when he arrived on the island of St Helena in 1882. He has lived there ever since.

54 years
The average life expectancy of a person born in Central African Republic in 2022. This is the lowest in the world.

Clam-ity

An ocean quahog – a type of clam – named Ming was estimated to be 507 years old after it was gathered from the seas around Iceland in 2006. This meant that it was born before Christopher Columbus sailed across the Atlantic. Unfortunately, it died while being examined.

122 years, 164 days
The age of the oldest confirmed person in the world, a French woman named Jeanne Calment (1875–1997).

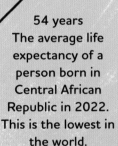

85 years
The average life expectancy of a person born in Hong Kong in 2022, the highest of any place in the world.

2,300 years
The oldest giant barrel sponges found in the Caribbean Sea were born before the start of the ancient Roman Empire.

4,855 years
A bristlecone pine tree in eastern California is estimated by scientists to have germinated from a seed in 2833 BCE – more than 200 years before the ancient Egyptians began work building the Great Pyramid.

SIGN OF THE TIMES

Through the centuries, many different styles and fashions have come and gone. Looking back, you can chart the passage of time by seeing which styles of architecture and clothing were in fashion at a certain point in history.

All Change!

Fashions can change quickly today, with mass media and the Internet allowing trends to be shared in seconds. But in the past, information spread far more slowly, and fashions might take a century to take hold in countries and continents.

New styles can emerge partly because of advances in how things are made or the discovery or invention of new materials, such as nylon and other artificial fibres for clothing, or plastics or concrete cast into curved shapes in architecture.

Fashions also change because of changes in society. In Europe a hundred years ago, for example, more and more women started riding bicycles and going to work, so fashions moved away from impractical billowing dresses and tight corsets. Later, World War Two brought demands for simpler clothes that used less fabric.

Timeline of Western Architecture and Fashion

Classical (c. 900 BCE – 470 CE)
Stone columns
Emphasis on symmetry

Gothic (1100–1450)
Pointed arches
Tall, slender towers

Baroque (1600s–1750)
Lavish detail and decoration
Curved shapes, domes and spires

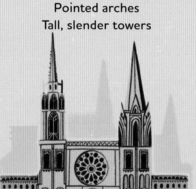

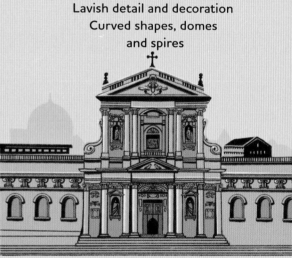

Ancient Rome
Toga worn by men of status

Ancient Greece
Loose, draped tunics

1300s Wool tunic and thick tights known as hose

1300s Long-sleeved, floor-length gown

1600s Doublet (jacket) and breeches

1600s Large collars and embroidered gowns

Revivals

Many clothes and architectural styles go out of fashion only to make a comeback or revival many decades or centuries later. Neoclassical architecture, which began in Europe in the 1700s, copied the columns, domes and symmetrical lines of ancient Greece and Rome's classical style. In Victorian Britain in the 1800s, a 'Gothic Revival' occured, inspired by the Gothic architecture of the medieval period. It resulted in buildings like the Houses of Parliament in London.

Clothing fashions may also take inspiration from earlier styles. Whilst platform shoes were a feature of the

glam-tastic 1970s, they were really a revival of a Renaissance invention called chopines. These tall wooden shoes started out as a practical way of raising women's dress bottoms above the muddy streets, but they quickly grew ridiculously tall. Some were 50 cm high and required servants to steady the wearer as they tottered down the streets.

Neoclassical (1730–1920s)
Greek and Roman-style columns and arches
A return to symmetry

Modernist (1900–present)
Box-shaped or abstract design
Concrete walls and big glass windows

Post-Modernist (1970s–present)
Playful designs. Use of new materials like plastics

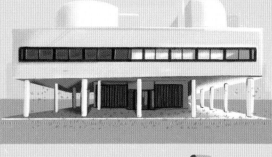

Early 1800s Simple, flowing dresses influenced by ancient Greece

1850s Long jackets and top hats for wealthy men

1850s Giant crinoline skirts

1920s Slim, simple flapper dresses

1930s Suit, tie and a fedora hat

1970s Flared trousers and colourful shirts

1980s Leggings and leg warmers

TIME OF YOUR LIFE

Even when you're just chilling out, there's a surprising amount going on inside and outside your body. Everybody's different, but these average figures give an idea of the amazing processes that take place every second, minute, hour, day and month you are alive.

In a Second

Your incredible body makes around 3.8 million new cells. Most of these are either blood cells or cells from your gut.

Food travels down your oesophagus toward your stomach a distance of 2–3 cm.

A single brain cell called a neuron can send up to 1,000 signals to other neurons. Your brain has millions of neurons, which adds up to lots of activity.

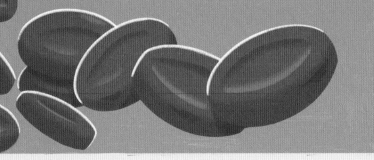

In a Minute

You'll breathe in around 16 times, each time drawing in 5–7 litres of air into your lungs.

Your eyes will gather in VAST amounts of visual information that is sent via the optical nerve to your brain. Your brain processes around 600 million bits of visual information during this time.

Whilst your brain is taking in all that information, your outer layers of skin are falling off. You shed at least 30,000 skin cells per minute.

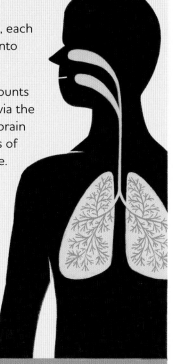

In an Hour

You will blink a staggering 800–1,200 times. Luckily, those little eyelid muscles have the stamina for the job.

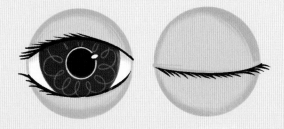

Pumped by your heart around your body, your blood travels a distance of 790 km.

You will have at least 50 separate thoughts.

In a Day

Your heart beats on average around 100,000 times, more if you have been really active. Each beat pumps about 70 ml of blood.

Your salivary glands will produce between 1 and 2 litres of drooling saliva, which helps you break down food in your mouth before it's swallowed.

You produce between 0.8 to 2 litres of urine a day. It is stored in a stretchy bag called the bladder in between visits to the toilet.

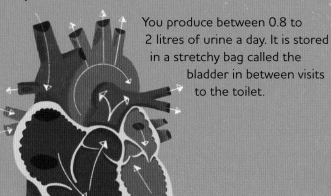

In a Month

A typical broken bone will be half or two-thirds of the way towards healing. Broken bones heal faster in children than they do in adults.

Your fingernails will grow around 3.5 mm. Your toenails grow more slowly, at about half that rate.

Hair on your head grows between 0.5 and 1.7 cm over this period. A typical head of hair has more than 100,000 individual hairs.

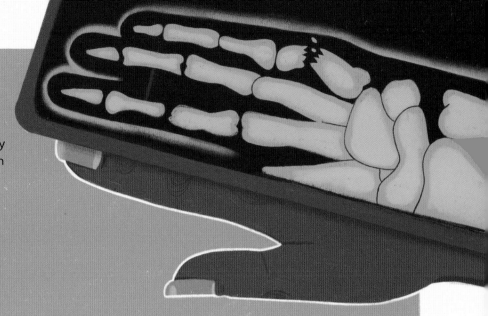

In a Lifetime

If life continues as it does today, then what does a typical person who reaches 79 years of age do with all those 28,854 days (including 19 leap years)?

An incredible 26 years will be spent asleep and up to 33 years in bed in total, resting, struggling to get up or trying to get to sleep.

As much as 11 years will be spent in front of a screen, be it TV, smartphone or tablet, either watching programmes or using the Web or social media.

You will spend around $4\frac{1}{2}$ years eating and at least 50 days of your life queueing, not to mention over 2 years of your life in the bathroom.

BODY CLOCKS

Did you know that you carry clocks with you wherever you go? They're inside you, made up of cells and substances that work together to control your body's patterns of eating, sleeping and other processes.

Directing the Day

Here's a typical adult body clock, but as everyone is slightly different, timings may vary.

Circadian Rhythms

Your body runs on a series of approximately 24-hour-long patterns or cycles known as circadian rhythms. They're partly responsible for the times you feel tired or energetic, hungry, alert or in need of a good sleep. Even your blood pressure and when you need to visit the toilet for a bowel movement may be controlled in this way.

21

9PM – MELATONIN RELEASED

6PM – HIGHEST BLOOD TEMPERATURE

18

Lots of Clocks

Most of the organs and tissues in your body have cells containing parts that help act as clocks or timers. A group of about 20,000 cells in your brain called the SCN (suprachiasmatic nuclei) act as a sort of master clock that sets the time for all the other clocks. It does this often, using chemical messengers called hormones. When there is less light, such as at night, the SCN orders a hormone called melatonin to be made and released in your body, which makes you feel drowsy. The SCN also reduces melatonin levels in the morning, so in theory you should be wide awake!

5PM – GREATEST MUSCLE STRENGTH

3PM – FASTEST REACTION TIME

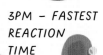

Larks and Owls

People's body clocks vary. Some people are 'morning larks', with body clocks instructing them to get up early and go to bed early. Others are the opposite and known as 'night owls'. A person's clock also changes throughout their life. A baby's clock tends to make it sleep for 14–20 hours a day, while a teenager's clock may be set an hour later than a typical adult's, which sees them want to stay awake longer and sleep in later.

15

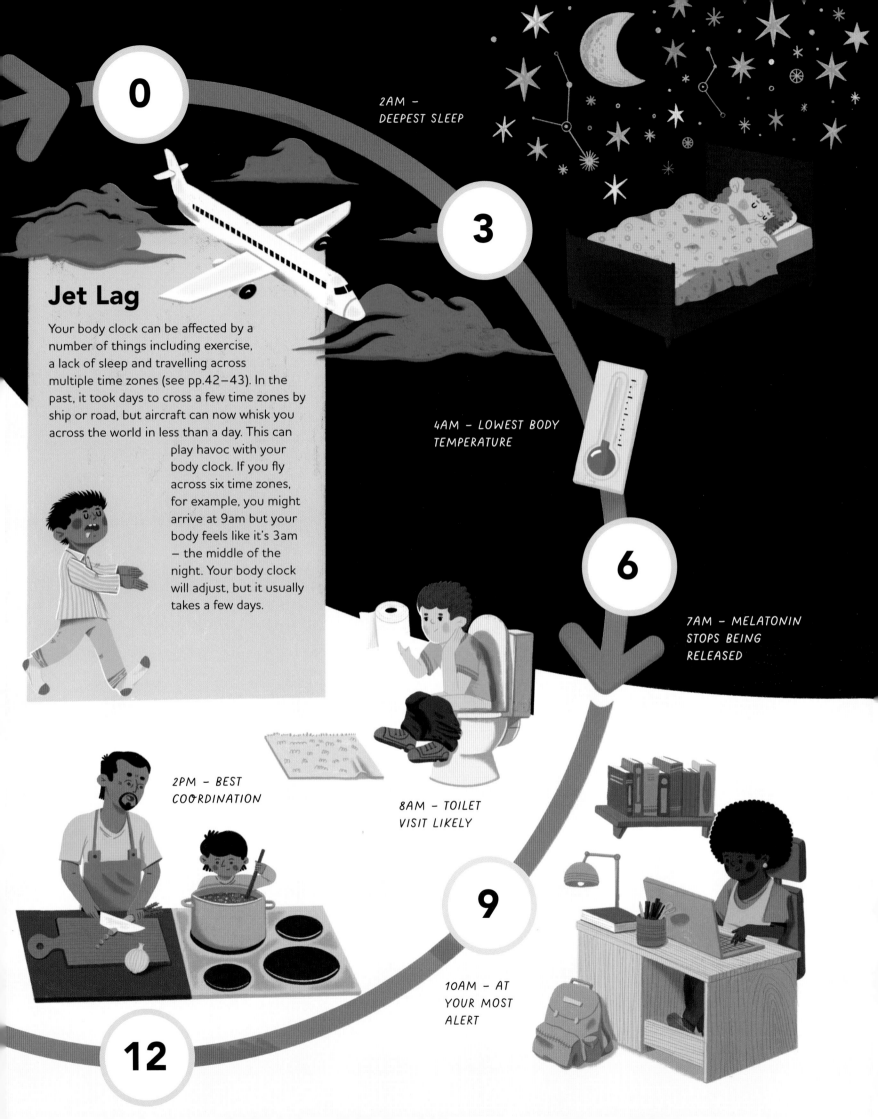

0

3

2AM – DEEPEST SLEEP

4AM – LOWEST BODY TEMPERATURE

6

7AM – MELATONIN STOPS BEING RELEASED

Jet Lag

Your body clock can be affected by a number of things including exercise, a lack of sleep and travelling across multiple time zones (see pp.42–43). In the past, it took days to cross a few time zones by ship or road, but aircraft can now whisk you across the world in less than a day. This can play havoc with your body clock. If you fly across six time zones, for example, you might arrive at 9am but your body feels like it's 3am – the middle of the night. Your body clock will adjust, but it usually takes a few days.

8AM – TOILET VISIT LIKELY

2PM – BEST COORDINATION

9

10AM – AT YOUR MOST ALERT

12

CAN ANIMALS TELL THE TIME?

Your dog can't tell you it's 11:15am and your cat doesn't know if it's Tuesday or that you're late for school. Scientists do believe, however, that many creatures can judge and measure time, some in ways quite different to us.

Mice on Time

Animals may be able to judge small amounts of time that pass. In a 2018 study, researchers trained mice to wait 6 seconds for a little door to open before they carried on their way for a treat. Later, when the door was removed, the mice still waited precisely 6 seconds before running on ahead. This shows that a part of their brain, connected to memory, is able to judge a set length of time.

Internal Clock

Just like humans, animals have body clocks (see p.60) and rely on changes in their body chemistry to tell them when to sleep and eat. The periodical cicadas, though, possess a particularly extreme internal timekeeper. These insects hatch from an egg into nymphs, burrow underground and stay buried for 17 years (or some species for 13 years), before popping up above ground to live for a few short weeks as adults. Quite how they know the right number of years still mystifies scientists.

AFTER MATING, THE FEMALE LAYS HER EGGS IN A SOFT TWIG

IT SHEDS ITS SKIN AND SPREADS ITS WINGS

17 YEARS LATER IT EMERGES FROM A HOLE

THE NYMPH LIVES UNDERGROUND, FEEDING ON TREE SAP

WHEN THE EGGS HATCH, THE TINY NYMPHS BURROW DEEP INTO THE SOIL AND THE CYCLE STARTS AGAIN

Quick Time, Slow Time

Small creatures tend to move, act and think very quickly as they experience smaller units of time to us. This creates the effect of time s l o w i n g down for them. A fly is so hard to swot because of the speed at which its eyes send visual information to its brain. Flies see far more frames of action every second than us (around 250 compared to our 60 or so). As a result, objects appear to them to be moving in super-slow motion compared to what we experience. This gives flies the chance to react quickly and buzz away from danger.

A DRAGONFLY SEES 300 FRAMES OF ACTION PER SECOND – EVEN MORE THAN A FLY! THIS HELPS MAKE THEM NATURE'S MOST LETHAL HUNTERS. THEY SUCCESSFULLY CAPTURE ABOUT 95% OF THEIR TARGETED PREY.

Time and Tide

The speckled sea louse tells the time by using sea tides. It knows when to bury itself deep in the sand to stop itself being washed away by waves and when it's safe to pop up above ground to look for food.

Oysters open and close their shells in time with certain phases of the Moon. Scientists think this may coincide with the movement of plankton that oysters feed on.

Changing Time

Swordfish are able to change the rate at which they perceive time. Normally, they see far fewer frames of action every second than humans (around one-fifth as many), so time appears to pass quickly. Before a swordfish goes off hunting, though, it pumps more blood to its eyes, where a special muscle heats it up by 10–15 °C. Warmer eyes means the swordfish's eyes send signals to its brain much more quickly. This seemingly slows down time, making it easier for the swordfish to spot quick flashes of movement that might be prey.

YOU'RE LATE!

We've all been late now and then, or suffered because of someone or something else's lateness. The first US President, George Washington, hated unpunctuality. He would start official dinners on time, bang on 4pm every Thursday, whether his guests had arrived or not!

Are You A Punctual Personality?

Unlike George Washington, some people are consistently late. Psychologists have grouped them into different personality types:

Perfectionist
Won't finish something or leave until everything, including how they look, is perfect.

Crisis maker
Loves the rush and drama of racing against time. Often feels more productive if under time pressure.

Defier
Chooses to be late to rebel against something, such as school or a family gathering.

Dreamer
Lives in a fantasy world, underestimates how long things take, and is easily distracted.

Unpunctual Punishments

Lateness costs businesses millions of pounds every year in delayed work, cancelled meetings and lost contracts. In some businesses, workers are fined if they're late regularly. In the Soviet Union in 1938, any worker who was more than 20 minutes late lost both their job and their government-supplied house. Harsh!

The 'Late' Emperor

In Qin Dynasty China, late government workers were sentenced to death and executed. In 209 BCE, this extreme punishment backfired when two army officers, Chen Sheng and Wu Guang, were delayed by rainstorms while marching 900 soldiers to Yuyang. Facing certain death and with nothing to lose, they began a rebellion. Soon, they had thousands of soldiers fighting with them. Although they were defeated, Chen and Wu inspired others to rebel and the Qin Emperor was overthrown not long after.

Time On Track

People and trains are expected to be on time in Japan... and usually are. Passengers on any Japanese train that is five or more minutes late can get a *chien shōmei sho* – a certificate of lateness – which they can show to their teacher or boss as proof it wasn't their fault!

Late But Lucky

Sometimes, just sometimes, late can be great. In 1862, gold prospector William 'Billy' Barker seemed to arrive late to a possible gold rush in Canada. Most of the best pieces of land had already been claimed, so Barker began mining some unpromising land by a creek... and struck gold! It turned out to be one of Canada's largest-ever gold hauls, worth tens of millions of pounds today.

Late Escape

In 1915, famous music composer Jerome Kern overslept and was too late to board the *Lusitania* cruise liner, which was sailing from New York to Europe. He was lucky. The ship was torpedoed by a submarine, killing most of the passengers and crew.

Long Overdue

Librarians curse late books, but few books have been later than one taken out of the New York Society Library in 1789 and only returned in 2010. The culprit, if still alive, would have technically owed more than £209,000 in library fines. Who was it?

None other than George Washington – the ever-so-punctual President of the United States!

RECORD TIMES

Time plays a big part in many world records. All sorts of timed records exist, both serious and silly. Let's take a look at some of the shortest, quickest, longest and slowest times in the record books.

Blink and you would miss Yusheng Du from China solving a Rubik's Cube in just 3.47 seconds in 2018. The fastest Rubik's Cube solve by a robot is even speedier — just 0.38 seconds!

In 2009, American David Slick juggled three balls continuously, without dropping a single one, for 12 hours and 5 minutes. That's enough time to play eight full football matches.

Are You a Record Breaker?

Why not try out these timed challenges with your friends to see who's the fastest. How do you compare to the world record holders? You'll need a stopwatch or stopwatch app on your phone.

CHECKMATE!

With chess pieces placed beside a chessboard, what's the quickest you can place all the pieces on their correct starting square?

World Record: 30.31 seconds — David Rush (USA) in 2021.

YOU'RE SORTED

Get someone to randomly shuffle a full pack of playing cards. How long does it take to arrange all the cards from Ace to King each in their correct suit?

World Record: 35.20 seconds - Lim Kai Yi (Malaysia) in 2022.

Ivan Scott from Ireland sheared an entire adult sheep of all its wool in 37.9 seconds — less than the time it sometimes takes to put a woolly jumper on!

HEADING UP

Try this challenge to keep two balloons in the air using just your head for the longest possible time.

World Record:
6 minutes, 43.7 seconds –
Dylan Demers (USA) in 2021.

TOILET TOWER

How quickly can you stack a tower of 10 toilet rolls using just one hand?

World Record:
5.45 seconds –
Silvio Sabba (Italy)
in 2019.

Some poor people don't volunteer to set a record. Poon Lim was a steward aboard a merchant ship during World War Two. When his ship sank in the Atlantic Ocean, he set an endurance record of 133 days at sea on a 2.4-m-long wooden raft before he was rescued. Lim survived by collecting rainwater and fishing.

Today, Olympic wrestling bouts are each 5 minutes long. But in the past, they continued until there was a winner. In a closely-fought contest at the 1912 Olympics, Russian wrestler Martin Klein took 11 hours and 40 minutes to defeat Alfred Asikainen from Finland. Klein was sadly too exhausted to take part in the next bout, which was for a gold medal.

In 2019, Sharofiddin Boltaboev from Uzbekistan won the quickest top-flight judo bout. He threw his opponent and was victorious in just 2.88 seconds at the Tashkent Grand Prix event.

LOUIS XIV

QUEEN ELIZABETH

In 2022 Queen Elizabeth II celebrated her 70th year on the British throne. It made her rule one of the longest in history, second only to King Louis XIV's 72-year, 110-day rule of France.

Another French king, Louis XIX, holds the record for the shortest rule – he was king for just 20 minutes before he abdicated!

LOUIS XIX

The *Karne Garibaldi* restaurant in the Mexican city of Guadalajara really puts the fast into fast food. It was timed by Guinness World Records as serving a meal in just 13 ½ seconds. In contrast, Bitto Storico cheese from Lombardy, Italy is often stored and aged for 18 years before it goes on sale – a long wait if you're hungry!

TIME SAVERS

Some people spend a lot of time complaining about how they have no time. Yet, if you live in a wealthy country today, you're surrounded by machines designed to save you time.

Travel Times

For thousands of years, the fastest way to travel was on horseback or by horse-drawn carriage. The development of steam trains in the 1820s speeded things up dramatically. Within 20 or 30 years, they were steaming along at 100 km per hour. Today's high-speed electric trains can travel four to five times further in 1 hour than a horse-rider could travel in a full day.

PRE-1900S: STAGECOACHES AVERAGE 10-20 KM/H BUT NEED A CHANGE OF HORSES OVER LONG DISTANCES.

1829: STEPHENSON'S ROCKET LOCOMOTIVE REACHES 46 KM/H.

1840S: STEAMSHIPS START CROSSING THE ATLANTIC IN 15–17 DAYS.

1886: KARL BENZ'S 'MOTORWAGEN' USHERS IN THE ERA OF PETROL-DRIVEN CARS.

1900: LARGE, POWERFUL CRUISE LINERS CROSS THE ATLANTIC IN 6-8 DAYS.

Line Time

In the past, most things were made slowly and painstakingly by hand, with one or several people working on every stage of construction until the item was complete. Early motor cars took days to make. Ransom Olds changed that with his 1902 car assembly line, in which workers only worked on one part of the car, doing the same task again and again.

Henry Ford took Olds' idea further, bringing the parts and cars to the workers using moving conveyor belts. The time taken to put together a Model T Ford car fell from 12–15 hours to 1 hour, 33 minutes! More than 15 million Model Ts were built.

Today most products are mass produced and assembled on lines, often using robots to save even more time.

Home savings

Electricity arrived in homes in the 20th century and with it, lots of time-saving appliances. The average US household spent 58 hours per week on housework in 1900. That had dropped to under 12 hours by 2019.

Before automatic washing machines, 'wash day' often took all day and meant scrubbing clothes by hand.

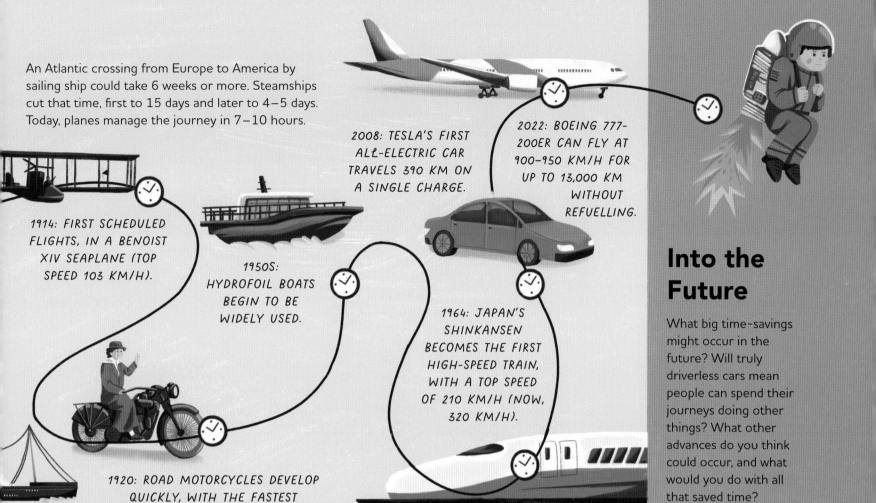

An Atlantic crossing from Europe to America by sailing ship could take 6 weeks or more. Steamships cut that time, first to 15 days and later to 4–5 days. Today, planes manage the journey in 7–10 hours.

1914: FIRST SCHEDULED FLIGHTS, IN A BENOIST XIV SEAPLANE (TOP SPEED 103 KM/H).

1950S: HYDROFOIL BOATS BEGIN TO BE WIDELY USED.

2008: TESLA'S FIRST ALL-ELECTRIC CAR TRAVELS 390 KM ON A SINGLE CHARGE.

2022: BOEING 777-200ER CAN FLY AT 900–950 KM/H FOR UP TO 13,000 KM WITHOUT REFUELLING.

1964: JAPAN'S SHINKANSEN BECOMES THE FIRST HIGH-SPEED TRAIN, WITH A TOP SPEED OF 210 KM/H (NOW, 320 KM/H).

1920: ROAD MOTORCYCLES DEVELOP QUICKLY, WITH THE FASTEST EXCEEDING 130 KM/H BY 1929.

Into the Future

What big time-savings might occur in the future? Will truly driverless cars mean people can spend their journeys doing other things? What other advances do you think could occur, and what would you do with all that saved time?

Fridge-freezers preserve foods for far longer, reducing the need to go shopping for fresh food daily.

Microwave ovens cook food in a handful of minutes.

Robot vacuum cleaners can clean most floors.

Super, Computers

You may moan at a slow-loading web page but computers have speeded up maths and data processing incredibly. One of the first digital computers, ENIAC, made in 1945, filled an entire large room. It calculated the flight paths of artillery shells – a task that took humans 12 hours, but ENIAC just 30 seconds.

Computers have slimmed down and speeded up since ENIAC's day. By 1997, all of ENIAC's abilities had been shrunk into a single microchip the size of your fingernail! Even if your smartphone is not the latest model, it's much faster than early computers. One supercomputer can do in a second what all the world's computers in 1960 would take months to process!

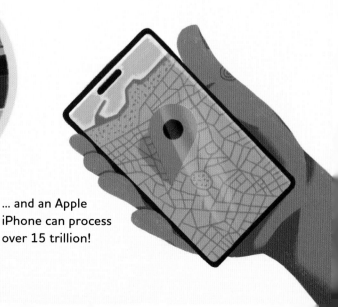

Humans can process just 1 instruction per second, while ENIAC could process 5,000 instructions per second...

... and an Apple iPhone can process over 15 trillion!

TIME WASTERS

We all waste time sometimes, idly lolling about when we could be doing something else more useful. But procrastination is major league time-wasting; it's the act of delaying or putting off tasks you know you should be doing.

Time Terrors

From social media to gaming or watching TV, there are so many wonderful ways to put off doing things we don't want to do. People procrastinate for different reasons, from fear of failing to being distracted by something more fun.

Some people enjoy putting themselves under mega-pressure by leaving everything until the last possible minute. Most, though, find looming deadlines for school, college or work can create guilt and stress. These can, in turn, make it harder to sleep and may cause anxiety and other health problems.

MAYA ANGELOU

Novel Solutions

Writers, especially, seem to find procrastination a problem. To avoid distractions, American writer Maya Angelou used to hire a sparse, small hotel room with bare walls. That's nothing, though, compared to American author, Herman Melville. He struggled so much to finish his epic whale of a novel, *Moby Dick*, that he got his wife to chain him to his desk so he couldn't wander away! French author Victor Hugo's dramatic solution when struggling to write *The Hunchback of Notre Dame* was to strip off and only have his clothes returned to him by a servant at the end of the day!

HERMAN MELVILLE

VICTOR HUGO

The Late Last Supper

You wouldn't necessarily think that a genius who designed bridges, parachutes and helicopters and produced the world's most famous painting – *Mona Lisa* – was a time-waster, but you'd be wrong. Italian artist and scientist Leonardo da Vinci was constantly getting distracted with new thoughts and would doodle constantly in his notebooks. The *Mona Lisa* is a small painting just 77 x 53 cm, but it took da Vinci 16 years to complete. In his 45-year career, he finished fewer than 20 artworks. One of these, *The Last Supper*, was only completed after much dawdling when the Duke of Milan threatened not to pay him!

The Blank Page

In 1934, American architect Frank Lloyd Wright agreed to design a family home. For a year, he then mostly procrastinated, until the client phoned to say he would visit later that day. The story goes that in just 2 hours, Wright and his assistants finished the design of Fallingwater – a house on top of a waterfall – that became an American icon. Phew!

Time To Shine

Even with a good night's sleep, meals and chores, you have plenty of precious hours to play with each day. Don't underestimate what you can do with them. Pablo Picasso could paint three paintings in a day, while Mozart only needed 4 days to compose an entire symphony, and Adele recorded the vocals to her hit song, *Skyfall*, in just 10 minutes.

You might not be the next Picasso, Mozart or Adele, or want to stop lazing about entirely, but you can use some of your time more wisely. Top tips for less procrastination and more action include:
• Break down a task into smaller, easy-to-do chunks.
• Place distractions, like smartphones, out of reach for a time.
• Don't think too far ahead – focus on the current part of the task.
• Reward yourself for completing a task.

PABLO PICASSO

THE TIME IT TAKES

In the time it takes to play any number-one hit single, you could complete the shortest commercial airline flight – a 90-second hop between the Scottish islands of Westray and Papa Westray. Let's look at some other surprising time comparisons.

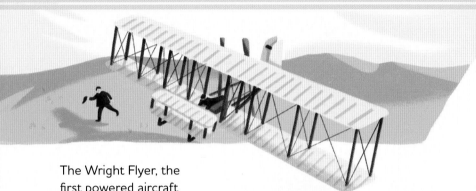

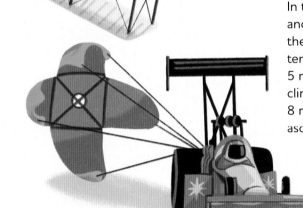

The Wright Flyer, the first powered aircraft flight, was only in the air for a mere 12 seconds. Still, that's more than four times longer than the first liquid-fuelled rocket flight by Robert Goddard in 1926 (2.5 seconds) and three times longer than a Top Fuel dragster race lasts (4 seconds).

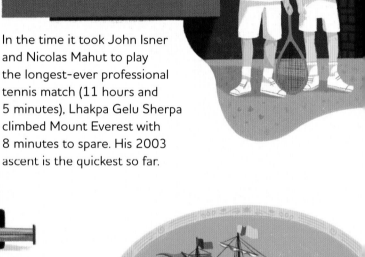

In the time it took John Isner and Nicolas Mahut to play the longest-ever professional tennis match (11 hours and 5 minutes), Lhakpa Gelu Sherpa climbed Mount Everest with 8 minutes to spare. His 2003 ascent is the quickest so far.

The first successful round-the-world voyage, began in 1519 and led by Ferdinand Magellan, took 1,082 days to complete. In that amount of time, Yuri Gagarin, the first person in space, could have travelled 14,426 times round the world in his Vostok 1 spacecraft. Gagarin's orbit of Earth took 1 hour, 48 minutes.

The longest world championship chess match (the 1984–1985 Karpov-Kasparov match) took 159 days. That's 26 $\frac{1}{2}$ times longer than it took Sweden's Markus Persson to create the first version of the famous computer game, Minecraft.

Some momentous events take a surprisingly short amount of time. The 1906 San Francisco earthquake lasted no more than 60 seconds yet tore down 500 city blocks and left half the city's people homeless. In half of that time, a cheetah has typically accelerated from a standstill to over 80 km/h, chased its prey and is already slowing down. Cheetahs rarely sprint at top speed for more than 20–30 seconds.

Samuel Beckett's *Breath*, first performed in 1969, is the world's shortest play. It lasts just 30 seconds – long enough for you to have been able to watch the world's oldest surviving film 14 times. The film, made in 1888 by French inventor Louis Le Prince, was called *Roundhay Garden Scene* and is just 2.11 seconds long.

BREATH and other shorts

SAMUEL BECKETT

In the 2 months it takes for your hair to grow approximately 2.5 cm, a baby blue whale can put on as much as 5,400 kg in weight – more than the weight of a monster truck.

The famous Empire State Building skyscraper in New York was completed in just 1 year, 45 days. Some weeks, five entire floors of the building were built in a week! Compare that to Italy's Leaning Tower of Pisa, which wasn't completed for 197 years. Building was interrupted by wars and head-scratching when the tower began leaning alarmingly.

Valeri Polyakov holds the record for the longest single space mission, spending 437 days and 17 hours on board the cramped Mir Space Station. In just a fifth of that time, Mark Beaumont cycled around the world in 2017, covering more than 29,000 km and cycling through 16 countries in under 79 days.

ONCE IN A LIFETIME

The Sun rising and setting is not the only phenomenon in nature that occurs regularly. Some natural events happen several times a day, but others are once-in-a-lifetime rarities.

Once Every Few Minutes

A shooting star can be viewed every 10–15 minutes across a clear sky at night. These are meteors – tiny pieces of space rock, metal or dust that burn up as they enter Earth's atmosphere.

Many geysers erupt in regular patterns, sending jets of hot water and steam high up into the air. America's Old Faithful geyser erupts every 35–120 minutes, almost without fail.

Once a Day

Many species of bats roost in caves or trees during the day and begin their night's hunting at sunset. This is seen at its most extreme at Bracken Cave, USA where some 15 million Mexican free-tailed bats roost during the summer. Every evening, they turn the sky black as they exit the cave.

Once Every 6 Months

A tidal bore sees the water flowing from a river into the sea reverse its direction and surge upstream instead. The Pororoca tidal bore on the Amazon River is at its strongest every equinox (in March and September). Powerful waves up to 4 m tall flow up the river as far as 800 km from the sea. Surfers can even ride the wave!

Once a Year

Many animal migrations occur annually, with creatures moving elsewhere to breed, escape harsh winters or reach new feeding grounds. Every year on Christmas Island, in the Indian Ocean, millions of bright red crabs migrate from the forest to the coast to breed, turning the ground red with their densely packed bodies.

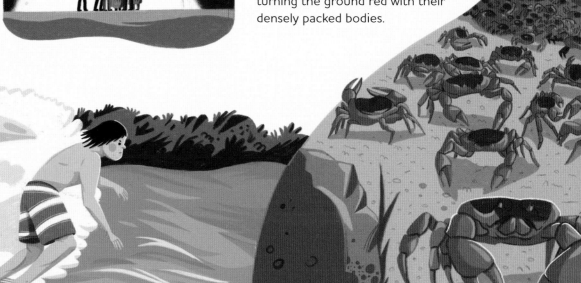

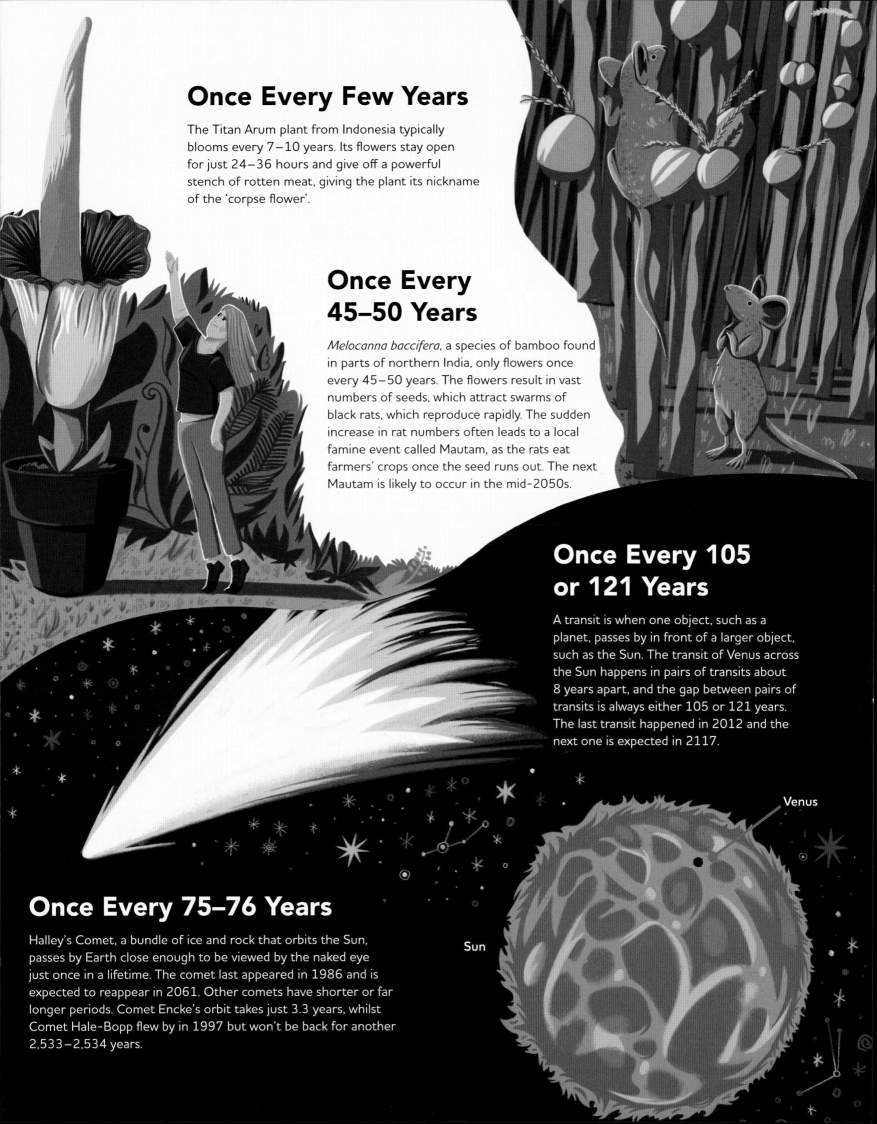

Once Every Few Years

The Titan Arum plant from Indonesia typically blooms every 7–10 years. Its flowers stay open for just 24–36 hours and give off a powerful stench of rotten meat, giving the plant its nickname of the 'corpse flower'.

Once Every 45–50 Years

Melocanna baccifera, a species of bamboo found in parts of northern India, only flowers once every 45–50 years. The flowers result in vast numbers of seeds, which attract swarms of black rats, which reproduce rapidly. The sudden increase in rat numbers often leads to a local famine event called Mautam, as the rats eat farmers' crops once the seed runs out. The next Mautam is likely to occur in the mid-2050s.

Once Every 105 or 121 Years

A transit is when one object, such as a planet, passes by in front of a larger object, such as the Sun. The transit of Venus across the Sun happens in pairs of transits about 8 years apart, and the gap between pairs of transits is always either 105 or 121 years. The last transit happened in 2012 and the next one is expected in 2117.

Venus

Once Every 75–76 Years

Halley's Comet, a bundle of ice and rock that orbits the Sun, passes by Earth close enough to be viewed by the naked eye just once in a lifetime. The comet last appeared in 1986 and is expected to reappear in 2061. Other comets have shorter or far longer periods. Comet Encke's orbit takes just 3.3 years, whilst Comet Hale-Bopp flew by in 1997 but won't be back for another 2,533–2,534 years.

Sun

TIME ON YOUR MIND

How time passes and how you think it passes can be two different things. It's one of many quirks involving you, your brain and time.

Poor Judges

Humans are good at judging short periods of time, like a handful of seconds, but not so good at longer durations. If nothing happens during a period of time, we overestimate how long it lasts. This can mean that when we're bored, time drags and feels like it is passing more slowly than it really is.

The opposite is also the case. When we are distracted by lots of interesting tasks and experiences, we tend to underestimate how long a period of time lasts. We may think just 15 minutes has passed, when it was really 20 or 25.

All in the Past

Everything you see, hear and experience is effectively already in the past. This is because there is a small delay of around 0.08 seconds from the moment something happens to the point at which your brain registers it. This is the time it takes for the signals to travel from your senses via your nerves to your brain and for your brain to analyse the information.

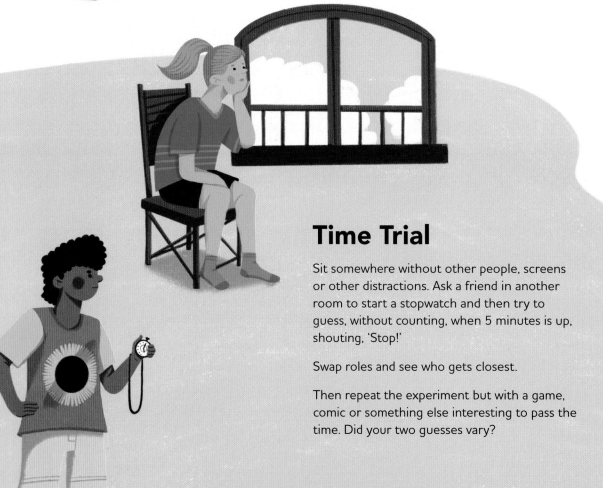

Time Trial

Sit somewhere without other people, screens or other distractions. Ask a friend in another room to start a stopwatch and then try to guess, without counting, when 5 minutes is up, shouting, 'Stop!'

Swap roles and see who gets closest.

Then repeat the experiment but with a game, comic or something else interesting to pass the time. Did your two guesses vary?

Memory Matters

You have two types of memory that operate over different timespans.

Short-term memory only lasts around 15–30 seconds, and can only hold 4–7 different thoughts or experiences at one time. If something is not thought about again, it will drop out of short-term memory and be gone.

If your brain pays attention to something in short-term memory, it may get moved into your long-term memory. This is held as connections between brain cells all over your brain. Long-term memories can last a lifetime.

Movies in Mind

The human eye and brain can only process so many images each second. An image stays on the back of the eye for a short period (about 1/30th of a second) before it is replaced by the next one. People learned how to exploit this to create the first animations and films. If a sequence of individual photos or drawings are shown one after another quickly enough (at least 12–15 images per second), people's brains mistake them as one continuous, moving image or movie.

Brain Biases

Your brain may favour or place more importance on certain things due to something called bias. 'Primacy bias' is the term used to describe how your brain is more likely to recall the first piece of information on a long list. 'Recency bias' is favouring things that you learned or experienced most recently.

Both biases can sometimes happen together! So, when someone gives you a long list of information, such as telling you all the meals on a menu or giving you detailed directions, chances are you will remember the first item on the list and the last few, but not those in the middle.

THE TIME, THE PLACE

From unique clocks and buried time capsules to countries where weekends take place on weekdays, these places around the world have a special connection to time.

Maine, USA
Jack Schoff had one of the biggest clock collections in the world, with 1,509 clocks of all shapes and sizes.

Oslo, Norway
Since 2014, 100 writers, one a year, will each donate an unpublished book manuscript to this time capsule. The books will remain unread until the capsule opens a century later, in 2114.

Nebraska, USA
The world's biggest time capsule contains 5,000 different objects, from coins and books to entire motor cars. Its opening date is 4th July, 2025.

Nevada, USA
At the 2011 Burning Man festival, three lasers shining on a circle of towers formed the world's largest-ever clock with a face 2.8 km wide! Each laser was an hour, minute or second hand and measured 1.6 km long.

Texas, USA
A giant mechanical clock that is designed to tell the time for 10,000 years is being built under a mountain. It will tick just once a year.

La Paz, Bolivia
Since 2014, the large clock on the front of the country's House of Congress has run backwards, to mimic the anti-clockwise direction that shadows move round a sundial in the southern hemisphere.

Amazon rainforest, Brazil
The Amondawa tribe have no words in their language for days, months or years. Instead of counting their age in years, people change their names to reflect different stages of their life.

St Petersburg, Russia
Peter Carl Fabergé's factory built incredible egg-shaped clocks for the rich and royals, which today sell for millions of pounds. Some are displayed at the Fabergé Museum in St Petersburg.

Thailand
This country uses two calendars: the Gregorian calendar for day-to-day life, and a lunar calendar called Patithin Chanthrakhati, which is used for traditional festivals and printed on birth certificates. This calendar is 543 years ahead, so 2024 for the rest of the world will be 2567 in Thailand!

Halberstadt, Germany
The longest piece of music in the world is being performed here. 'ORGAN²/As Slow As Possible' by John Cage began in 2001 and won't finish until the year 2640!

Somalia
This is one of the few countries where Thursday and Friday are considered to be the weekend. Yemen used to be the same, but in 2013, it changed to a Friday and Saturday weekend.

Jaipur, India
The world's largest stone sundial, the Samrat Yantra, is 27 m tall. The shadow it casts moves at a rate of 6 cm every minute.

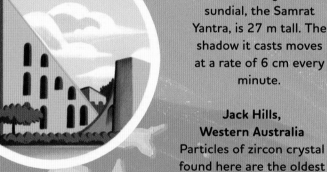

Jack Hills, Western Australia
Particles of zircon crystal found here are the oldest known thing on Earth – 4.4 billion years old !

Cape Town, South Africa
A cannon has been fired here at precisely noon since 1806. Today, it even has a Twitter account, which tweets 'Boom!' every day at noon.

Antarctica
In 2017, scientists managed to bore an ice core that contained 2.7-million-year-old ice layers, the oldest in the world.

THE FOURTH DIMENSION

Every object and empty space has three dimensions: length, width and height. Scientists used to think of time as its own dimension, separate from three-dimensional space. But Albert Einstein and his old teacher changed that view forever.

Welcome to Space-time

Hermann Minkowski was a German maths professor who had been one of Albert Einstein's teachers in the 1890s. In the 1900s, he drew inspiration from his old pupil to show how time and space were part of the same thing, called a space-time continuum. Minkowski believed that you cannot consider movement through space without considering movement through time as well.

After all, travelling on a cross-country road trip isn't just a journey through space from your starting point to your destination. It's also a journey through time, as the trip takes hours or minutes to complete.

Graphic Thinking

Minkowski developed graphs and diagrams to show space-time. The simplest 2D graph placed all three dimensions of space on one graph axis and time on the other axis. Even something that stands stock still, like a kitchen fridge, still moves through time, so scientists can plot this along the graph's time axis.

Fridge stays still but time moves on

TIME

SPACE

Dog moves, changing its position in space over time

Car moves faster than dog, covering more space in the same time

Viewing stars and galaxies is a journey back in time. An image taken of the Andromeda galaxy today actually shows us how it looked 2.5 million years ago.

Relativity Speaking

In 1905, Einstein unveiled the first of his theories about relativity, with his second theory coming in 1916. These showed how space and time were linked and could be flexible.

Einstein showed that the speed of light was always the same, a whopping 299,792,458 metres travelled every second. Time and space, however, were both relative, which meant they could be s t r e t c h e d or squeezed in some circumstances. Time, according to Einstein, occurred at different rates depending on how fast an object was moving. At speeds close to light, time was s t r e t c h e d and would pass more slowly.

Space is squeezed at speeds close to the speed of light.

Warp Factor

Einstein believed that space-time could be curved or warped by massive objects (things like stars with huge amounts of stuff packed in them). A good way to think of this is to imagine space-time as a huge rubber sheet and the Sun or another massive star as a heavy bowling ball.

An object with a lot of mass pulls the sheet down, denting and warping space-time. Rolling a marble close by would see the marble pulled towards the warp in the space-time sheet. Einstein argued that this warping created the gravity that holds planets in orbits around stars.

Einstein's ideas changed how people viewed time and the way the Universe works. This led to some interesting ideas about speeding up time and the possibility of time travel (see next page). Not bad for someone who never learned to swim and hated wearing socks!

TIME TRAVEL

You're already sort of a time traveller, as you're always moving through time, with each minute that passes bringing the future nearer to the present. Real time travel is the ability to travel faster than the current rate of time passing, so that you reach some point in the distant future.

Time Dilation

One of the fascinating results of Einstein's work on space-time and relativity was that time moves slower as you move faster, especially if you move fast enough to get close to the speed of light. Vast amounts of the pulling force of gravity can also slow time. This very complicated area of physics is called time dilation.

So far, we have only achieved the teensiest amount of time dilation. In 2015–16, NASA astronaut Scott Kelly spent 11 months aboard the International Space Station (ISS) whilst his twin brother, Mark, stayed on Earth. Because the ISS was whizzing around Earth at high speed, Scott came back 0.013 seconds younger than his brother.

Speed It Up

The ISS is whizzing along at 27,600 km/h. Light in comparison travels at 1.07 billion km/h. If we were able to travel very close to the speed of light, time dilation would have a big effect. Imagine you're a 10-year-old astronaut on a 2-year mission aboard a spaceship able to travel at 99.9% the speed of light. When you return to Earth you'd be 2 years older, but it would be more than 40 years later on Earth. You've travelled to the future – well done! Every one of your 10-year-old friends would now be in their fifties.

2023

2063

Space Slowcoaches

The challenges in building a time machine able to travel at almost light speed are close to impossible at the moment. Our fastest machine, the Parker Solar space probe, is fast, but is still only 0.05% of the speed of light. Is there another way we could time travel? Some scientists think so, especially if space-time is curved.

Wormholes

A wormhole is a potential tunnel acting as a short cut between two places in space-time. Wormholes would each have an entrance, an exit and a narrow throat joining the two. If space-time is curved and folded back on itself in places, wormholes might exist and provide a quick way of time travelling. They might allow us to nip between two distant locations in space in moments that would otherwise have taken millions of years.

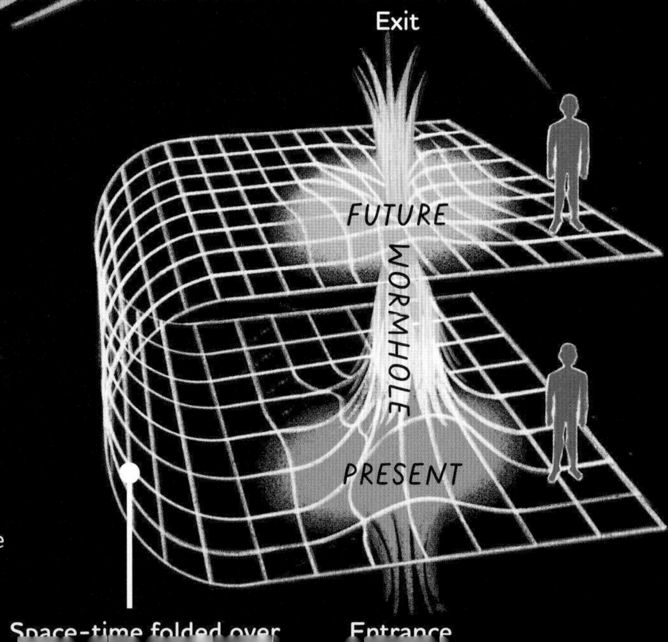

Exit

FUTURE

WORMHOLE

PRESENT

Space-time folded over   Entrance

Albert Einstein and Nathan Rosen came up with the idea of wormholes in 1935 (they are sometimes called an Einstein-Rosen bridge). Scientists believe they could exist in theory but none have yet been found. Even if they do exist, it might not be possible to pass through them unharmed. Still, they're a tremendously exciting idea. Where in time and space would you like your wormhole to take you to?

PUZZLES AND PARADOXES

Don't get too hasty and start planning your time travelling trip quite yet! There are many barriers in its way. Some of these involve problems in logic known as paradoxes, for which we don't have easy answers.

Cause and Effect

Is travelling back in time remotely possible? Could you meet your younger self and what impact could that have? Some people think it would simply create too many problems, such as how things cannot exist in two places at once.

Other thinkers argue that the Universe only works if time always moves forwards so that cause and effect can work. Scientists believe that things have causes – they don't happen on their own – which create effects, in that order. So, if a ball moves (the effect), the cause (the ball being kicked) must have occurred before. But time travel throws up the possibility of causes from the future creating effects in the past. Some believe this simply doesn't make sense and wouldn't be possible.

Fermi Paradox

This paradox wonders: 'Why haven't we encountered any aliens if there are so many billions of likely planets in the Universe?' But it can be applied to time travel as well. If travel backwards into the past is possible, why haven't time travellers from the distant future come to visit us?

Grandparent Paradox

This problem starts with you whizzing back in time to when your grandparents were alive but before they had brought your mother or father into the world. What if you accidentally killed your grandmother? Surely, that would mean that your family line would vanish, your own birth would be impossible and that would mean the end of you? And here's the head-spinning paradox bit... If, as a result, you weren't born in the future, then how could you have gone back to the past to kill your grandparent in the first place?

1. Build a time machine

2. Travel back in time to meet grandparents before they have children

3. Accidentally kill grandmother

4. Time traveller not born

5. Time machine not built

NO! THIS IS THE LAST DODO!

Ending Trouble

Another paradox involves a time traveller going back in time to stop something bad happening, such as an action by a terrible person. Removing the trouble, though, creates a problem. Back in their present world, the time traveller wouldn't have any knowledge about the terrible event because it would no longer have happened. So, they have no reason for travelling back in time in the first place.

Bootstrap Paradox

Imagine you travelled back in time to give a young William Shakespeare your copy of his play, *Macbeth*, to save him the trouble of writing it. Shakespeare then publishes your copy of *Macbeth* as his own work. So, now, who really wrote that original play? It no longer has an author! The play is caught in a loop with no starting point and without ever having been really created. Mind-numbing, isn't it?

THE FUTURE

No one's certain what the future has in store but that doesn't stop people from guessing!

Forecasting the Future

In order to predict what may happen in the future, people build models of how things have worked using data from the past. Many of the world's most powerful computers, known as supercomputers, run huge simulations of weather systems, hurricanes, earthquakes and diseases to try to make predictions or educated guesses about future threats.

Because things sometimes change in ways we cannot foresee, these models are not always spot on. In the US, for example, 7-day weather forecasts are correct up to 80% of the time.

Poor Predictions

Businesses and investors try to predict the future. Some get it right and make billions, but other predictions have made some very smart people look very foolish!

'The horse is here to stay, but the automobile is only a novelty.' – The president of an American bank to the Ford motor company, in 1903.

There are now more than 1 billion cars on the world's roads.

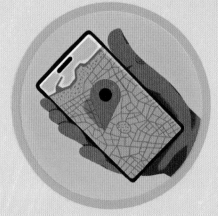

'There is no reason an individual would ever want a computer in their home.' – Ken Olsen, founder of DEC (a computing company), in 1977.

Ken was proven wrong with the invention of personal computers, laptops and tablets.

'Before man reaches the Moon, your mail will be delivered within hours from New York to Australia by guided missiles.' – Arthur Summerfield, US Postmaster General, in 1959.

Humans stood on the Moon just 10 years later, but your mail is still delivered on foot or by van.

'Rock n' roll? It'll be gone by June.' – *Variety* showbusiness magazine in 1955.

It had only just begun!

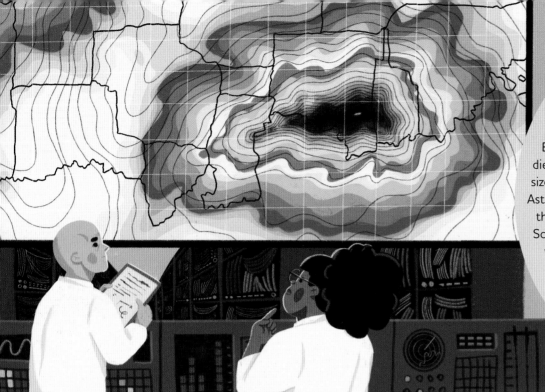

Time's Up!

Will time ever end? No one knows. Time will run out for Earth when the Sun begins to die and swells up to such a huge size that it will engulf our planet. Astronomers estimate, though, that this is at least 5 billion years away. So, you can relax. And time won't stop when the Earth does. It has already continued long after other planets and stars have disappeared. It would take the Universe to stop existing for time to end, and no one is predicting that will happen any time soon!

Futurology

Some writers have had startling success with their predictions, few more so than English writer H.G. Wells. Writing in the 1890s and 1900s, he predicted tanks, lasers, people landing on the Moon, emails and nuclear power. Quite some achievement! Professional futurists today study new inventions, advances and trends, trying to predict which will become popular and how they might change people's lives.

Amongst their predictions for 2050 or so are:

Floating warehouses and factories located offshore so they don't waste land.

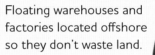

Changing diets include insects as a healthy source of protein.

Artificial intelligence (AI) medical booths – no need to see a human doctor.

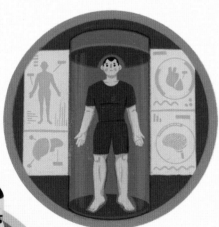

Driverless vehicles are everywhere.

Smart clothing monitors your health and can change colour and shape at command.

What do **you** think the future will be like? How will people live? Will there be new foods? Will people ride around on hoverboards? Why not get you and your friends to write down your own predictions.

A TIMELINE OF TIME

Time has been studied, tinkered with and inspired many inventions for thousands of years. Let's take a final look back at some of the biggest moments in the history of time.

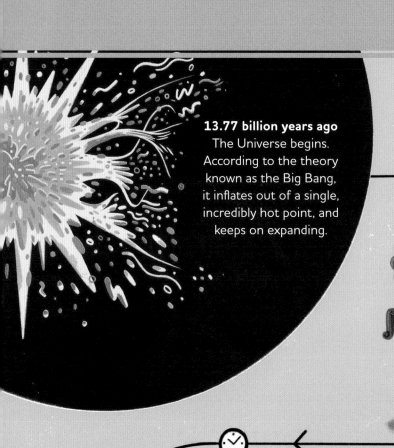

13.77 billion years ago
The Universe begins. According to the theory known as the Big Bang, it inflates out of a single, incredibly hot point, and keeps on expanding.

4.54 billion years ago
Our planet, Earth, begins to form.

3200 BCE
The Newgrange monument is built by Stone Age farmers in Ireland. It is aligned with the winter solstice to shine light into a passageway.

2100 BCE
The Babylonians' calendar has 354 days divided into 12 months. They also introduce 7-day weeks. The ancient Egyptians of the same era use 10-day weeks instead.

3100 BCE
The Sumerians in Mesopotamia (present-day Iraq) invent one of the first organised calendars, based on the cycles of the Moon.

1500 BCE
The oldest known sundial is used in ancient Egypt. It has a series of angled lines which, when shadow falls on one of them, indicates a time of the day.

400 BCE
The Ancient Greeks and Babylonians make and use water clocks that use the flow of water out of a large vessel to measure time.

1582
Pope Gregory XIII decrees that everyone should use the Gregorian calendar instead of the Julian calendar.

1656
Christiaan Huygens invents the first practical pendulum clock.

1519
Ferdinand Magellan sets sail on the first successful round-the-world voyage. Each of the five ships in his fleet carry 18 hourglasses for measuring time during the trip.

1505
German locksmith Peter Henlein makes small, portable clocks that can be worn around the neck or on clothing – the forerunner of the watch.

1386
The first recorded mention of the world's oldest surviving mechanical clock, still working in Salisbury Cathedral, UK.

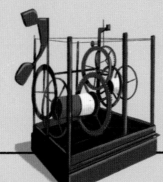

1482–1499
Leonardo da Vinci writes his *Treatise on Painting*, in which he mentions that trees form rings every year and their thickness depends on their growing conditions.

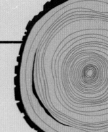

1027
Persian doctor and thinker, Ibn Sînâ writes *The Book of Healing*. In the book he describes how rocks form in layers with younger rocks on top of older ones – the basis of geological time.

725 CE
Buddhist monk Yi Xing invents a water clock that moves a large wheel around to complete a full revolution, once every 24 hours. The bronze and iron mechanism rings a bell every hour and beats a drum every quarter hour.

45 BCE
The new 365-day Julian calendar is adopted in ancient Rome and spreads through Europe.

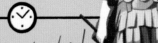

400 CE
People in Ethiopia develop a calendar still used by some today. It's split into 13 months and currently runs 7 years behind the Gregorian calendar used by most of the rest of the world.

520 CE
The earliest known reference to candle clocks is made in a poem by Chinese writer, You Jiangu. He described 30-cm-tall candles that burned down in 4 hours.

1712
A bit of a calendar mishap means that Sweden has to add two leap days in the same year. So, for one year only, 30th February becomes a real date in the Swedish calendar.

1740s
The first cuckoo clocks are built in the Black Forest region of Germany. On the hour, wooden cuckoo birds spring out of the clocks.

1761
John Harrison's H4 marine chronometer is tested at sea. It's proven to be accurate and helps sailors navigate at sea by finding longitude.

1832
The estimated year of birth of Jonathan, a Seychelles giant tortoise who in 2022, celebrated his 190th birthday.

1814
The Clockmakers' Collection is established in London. It is the oldest collection of clocks and watches in the world, with more than 1,250 timepieces.

1847
Antoine Redier from France becomes the first to invent and patent an adjustable alarm clock.

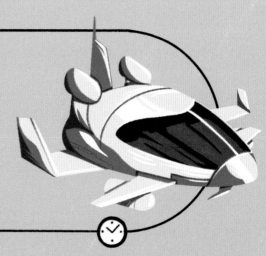

1878
Canadian engineer Sir Sandford Fleming proposes everyone use a 24-hour clock and a system of worldwide time zones.

1916
Albert Einstein completes his theory of relativity, which states that movement and gravity can distort time. It blows many people's minds and triggers much research and thought.

1895
The Time Machine, written by H.G. Wells, is published. This science fiction book popularises the idea of time travel.

1927
Two researchers at Bell Labs in the United States build a watch that uses a vibrating piece of quartz crystal to keep time.

1929
Soviet Union leader Joseph Stalin abolishes weekends to improve factory production. It's not a popular move!

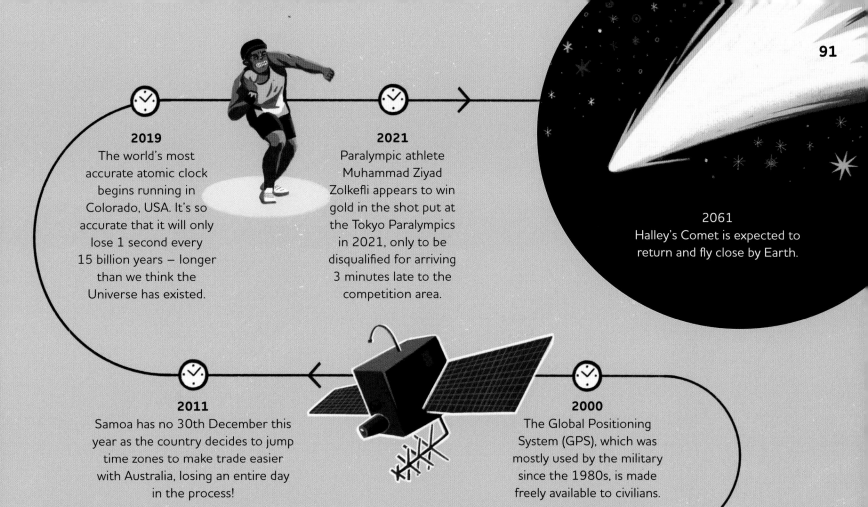

2019
The world's most accurate atomic clock begins running in Colorado, USA. It's so accurate that it will only lose 1 second every 15 billion years – longer than we think the Universe has existed.

2021
Paralympic athlete Muhammad Ziyad Zolkefli appears to win gold in the shot put at the Tokyo Paralympics in 2021, only to be disqualified for arriving 3 minutes late to the competition area.

2061
Halley's Comet is expected to return and fly close by Earth.

2011
Samoa has no 30th December this year as the country decides to jump time zones to make trade easier with Australia, losing an entire day in the process!

2000
The Global Positioning System (GPS), which was mostly used by the military since the 1980s, is made freely available to civilians.

1972
The Hamilton Pulsar goes on sale as the world's first digital watch. It sells for US$2,100 – about the same price as a small car at the time!

1975
The world's largest time capsule is sealed up in Nebraska, USA, to be opened in 2025.

1967
At a conference in Paris, time becomes atomised. A second is now defined as a number of vibrations of a Caesium atom – a whopping 9,192,631,770 of them.

1955
The first practical atomic clock is unveiled. It is accurate to 1 millisecond a day – equal to 1 second in about 300 years and a great advance at the time.

1946
American chemistry professor Willard Libby proposes radiocarbon dating as a way to check the age of formerly living things.

1949
The first atomic clock is created by United States National Institute of Standards and Technology (NIST). It is less accurate than scientific quartz clocks but proves that atomic clocks could work.

GLOSSARY

Ancient Egypt A civilisation that began around 5,000 years ago along the Nile River in northeast Africa, and lasted for over 3,000 years.

astronomer A scientist who studies outer space, including stars, planets, galaxies and comets.

atom The basic building block for all matter in the Universe. Everything is made of atoms, including you.

atomic clock An extremely accurate clock that measures time using the natural vibrations of atoms.

axis An imaginary line that runs through the centre of Earth from the North Pole to the South Pole. Earth spins on its axis, completing one rotation every 24 hours.

Aztecs A civilisation that ruled a large empire in what is now central Mexico, in the 15th and 16th centuries.

Babylonians People in the Babylonian Empire, which emerged in around 1,800 BCE in southern Mesopotamia (modern-day Iraq).

body clock A system in the human body that keeps track of time and controls automatic behaviour such as when you feel sleepy or hungry.

Byzantines The Byzantine Empire, which emerged after the Roman Empire split into two in 476 CE – the eastern part became the Byzantine Empire. It lasted until 1453.

cell Small structures that make up every living thing. Some (such as bacteria) are just one cell, while others (like humans) are made of trillions.

civilisation A large group of people who share a particular way of life.

digital clock A clock that shows the time using digits (for example, "2.28" or "17.32"), rather than hour and minute hands on a clock face.

equator The imaginary line that runs around the centre of the Earth, midway between the North Pole and the South Pole. It divides the Earth into the northern hemisphere and the southern hemisphere.

equinox The two times a year – in March and October – when day and night are around the same length, in both the northern and southern hemispheres.

GPS (Global Positioning System)
A network of 31 satellites that help determine the position of an object on Earth.

Greenwich Mean Time (GMT)
The time at the Royal Observatory in Greenwich in London, UK. The imaginary line that runs through Greenwich from the North Pole to the South Pole is called the Prime Meridian line.

Gregorian calendar The calendar used in most parts of the world today. It was introduced in Europe from the 16th century onwards.

hemisphere See *equator*

hourglass An instrument for measuring time, made up of two connected glass compartments, the upper of which is filled with sand. It takes an hour for the sand to flow from the upper to the lower compartment.

ice cap A thick layer of snow and ice that covers a large area, for example at the North and South Poles.

International Space Station (ISS) A space station orbiting Earth, which launched in 1998 and has been built in several stages by many different countries. Astronauts visit to perform tests and experiments.

Julian calendar The calendar introduced by Julius Caesar in 45 BCE, with 365 days divided into 12 months. It was used in most of the Western world until it was replaced by the Gregorian calendar.

Maya A civilisation that thrived in Mesoamerica (modern-day Mexico and Central America) between around 1000 BCE and 1600 AD.

mechanical Made or operated by a machine or machinery.

microchip A tiny device made up of electronic circuits, which drives computers, smartphones, appliances and other electronic systems.

migration The seasonal movement of animals from one place to another, for example to find food or to mate.

molecule Two or more atoms joined together. For example, a hydrogen molecule is made from two hydrogen atoms joined together.

North Pole The northernmost point of Earth, at the northern end of the planet's axis. The North Pole is located in the Arctic.

orbit The regular path that one object in space takes around another, for example the Moon around Earth, or Earth around the Sun.

pendulum A weight attached to a wire or string, hung from a fixed point.

philosopher A person who studies basic ideas about human life, such as knowledge, religion, and right and wrong.

polar Relating to the North Pole or the South Pole or the areas around them.

prehistoric Relating to the period of history before human beings could write.

psychologist A scientist who studies the human mind.

radioactive A property of some types of atoms, which change (or 'decay') over time and release small particles and energy as radiation.

Royal Observatory (Greenwich) An astronomical observatory in London, England, set up in 1675 to study the stars, navigation and timekeeping.

satellite A small object that orbits a larger object in space. Satellites launched into orbit around Earth are used for many purposes, including navigation and communication.

South Pole The southernmost point of Earth, at the southern end of the planet's axis. The North Pole is located in the Antarctic.

space probe A satellite that is sent to explore space and gather scientific information.

Sumerians One of the first great civilisations, which flourished in southern Mesopotamia (modern-day Iraq). It began around 6,000 years and lasted for over 2,000 years.

sundial An instrument that tells the time using the shadow cast by the Sun. As the Sun moves across the sky, the shadow of a pointer moves across a dial marked with the hours of the day.

time capsule A container filled with present-day objects and records, which is hidden away or buried, to be opened at some point in the future.

time zones Regions on Earth in which the same standard time is used. All of the world's time zones are measured from Greenwich Mean Time.

Universe Everything that exists, including living things, planets, stars, light and time.

water clock An instrument for measuring time, using the flow of water from one container to another.

World War One A war fought between 1914 and 1918 between many countries around the world, including much of Europe, the USA, Russia and Japan.

World War Two A war fought between 1939 and 1945 between the Axis powers (Germany, Italy and Japan) and the Allies (United Kingdom, USA, Soviet Union and France). The war involved many other countries around the world.

INDEX